THRESHOLD OF THE FUTURE

For Athol Gill,
who laughed and dreamed among us.

Other books by Mike Riddell

Fiction
The Insatiable Moon, Flamingo, 1997

Non-fiction
Godzone, Lion, 1992
Alt.Spirit@Metro.M3, Lion, 1997

THRESHOLD
OF THE
FUTURE

Reforming the Church
in the post-Christian West

-

MICHAEL RIDDELL

First published in Great Britain 1998
Society for Promoting Christian Knowledge
Holy Trinity Church
Marylebone Road
London NW1 4DU

Second Impression 1999

British Library Cataloguing-in-Publication Data
A catalogue record for this book is available from
the British Library

ISBN 0-281-05055-4

Typeset by David Gregson Associates, Beccles, Suffolk
Printed in Great Britain by The Cromwell Press

Contents

—

100496

CONTENTS

Introduction: Sick to Death

—

The Christian church is dying in the West. This painful fact is the cause of a great deal of avoidance by the Christian community. To use terminology drawn from pastoral care, the terminally sick patient is somewhere between denial and bargaining. Many refuse to contemplate the prospect of death, bolstered by small outbreaks of life, or encouraging one another to falsify the diagnosis. Others try to broker a deal with God, whereby if they remain faithful or pray harder or open themselves to a new experience, their small corner of congregational life will be saved.

In the face of painful realities, denial is a very human reaction. But as pastoral carers and theologians know, it is not a healthy state to remain in. Walter Brueggemann[1] has helped us to see that the starting point of moving on with God is a deep and heartfelt grief. It is not until we accept reality, however unpleasant it might be, that we can hope for change. For many years now, as a pastor and a theologian, I have watched the Western church fighting to repress the signs of its own demise.

It might be argued that I am overstating the case; that the Western church is simply having a bad day, and that all will come right eventually. Surely God will not let his church come to death? And yet the history of the church in North Africa teaches us that we cannot assume divine intervention to maintain the status of the ecclesiastical institution. It is not only possible for Christianity in the West to falter, it is apparent that the sickness is well advanced. The evidence is there to be seen, and I will survey some of it to build my case.

The recognition that we are blind and poor and naked is the beginning of hope. The purpose of this book is not to plunge the church into despair. Rather it is to call the

1

community of Christ back to its radical roots and its essential character as a missionary body. The current malaise is the result of clearly identifiable historical developments and compromises by the institutional church, and is largely self-deserved.

The deeper truth, I believe, is that God is substantially involved in the present crisis faced by the church. I am convinced we have been exposed by God to the cold winds of the twentieth century in order to call us forward. It is a moment of decision and extreme risk, when the community of Christ must slough off its previous paradigm of life in order that the new may emerge. In grappling with this transitional time, my own reflection has been driven back to some foundational texts of Scripture, themselves forged out of crisis situations.

This is a time which calls for courage and experimentation. Every crisis has elements of threat and opportunity. It is only when the full extent of the threat has been contemplated that it becomes possible to grasp the opportunity.[2] In the midst of crisis, people are often tempted to go back or to prevaricate. But it soon becomes apparent that there is no way back, and that to remain static is to die. The will to life requires moving onward and into the painful realities which the crisis represents, and making such changes as are necessary to flourish in a new environment. I think that this is the call of God to the Western church at the end of the second millennium: to change or to die.

So What's the Problem?

If there is a sickness unto death for the Western church as claimed here, the specific symptoms of the crisis need to be iterated. One qualification is perhaps necessary. It is my perception that the United States of America is less secularized than other parts of the West. In such places as Britain, France and Australasia, the decay of the church is advanced and more easily recognized. In Northern America, the high figures of church attendance and the engrained civil religion with its strong cultural element mean that the writing is not so clearly on the wall. This does not mean that the American church is any less bankrupt than its Western colleagues, but simply that American Christians might not so readily recognize the fact.

The following indicators are not exhaustive, but they do give the general outlines of what is a substantial crisis for the church.

THE CHURCH'S HAEMORRHAGE

According to David Barrett,[3] 53,000 attenders are leaving the church in Europe and North America every week, and they are not coming back. This exodus of believers is in itself a crisis of major proportions. Any business which was losing clients at this rate would be doing some serious reconsidering of its method and objectives. Because of the denominational fragmentation bequeathed by the Reformation, however, it is possible for the church to ignore the consequences. The reshuffling of allegiances among Christians helps to promote the illusion that at least some sections of the church are growing.

Why are people leaving? For a variety of reasons, some of which point to the underlying condition of the Christian community. Perhaps the easiest explanation for congregational exodus is the relaxation of societal sanction in regard to church-going. The post-war period seemed to induce a new sense of responsible freedom in those who had returned from hell. There was a readiness to question authority and make responsible choices; no longer to be dictated to by 'convention'. The concept of 'duty' in relation to civic and cultural agendas has diminished as an active force in guiding behaviour.

A related factor is the demise of the 'sabbath' concept. Previous generations in apparently Christian countries had reserved Sunday as the sole province of the church. For church attenders this meant fairly severe restrictions on what types of activities might be engaged in on that day. While the mindset of Christendom prevailed, civic authorities reinforced the church's pietism by regulating what might and might not take place on a Sunday. Many activities such as shopping, sports, drinking and entertainment were proscribed by law.

With the fragmentation of Christendom, the external strictures were gradually relaxed. In many parts of the formerly Christian West, there has been a reclamation of Sunday by those pastimes which had been excluded. In my home country of New Zealand, shopping has become a huge Sunday enterprise. Major sports games are regularly played on this day, with a shifting preference from Saturday for many lower-grade sporting events. Although alcohol restrictions remain in place, the exceptions have meant that there are a wide variety of entertainment options available on a Sunday.

In the face of this, and with discretional time at a premium for many people, church attendance has become one option among many. Unfortunately for the church, when the worship service is compared to the other possibilities on offer, it fails to stimulate the imagination of the populace at large. The pressures are felt keenly by families who struggle to maintain contact and communication in the context of competing demands. It is perhaps not surprising that some parents feel there is more to be gained by supporting their children's sports events or even going together to the shopping mall, than by enforcing attendance at church.

Hopes that the development of technology in the twentieth century would produce a dividend in the form of increased leisure time have not been realized. Those who have employment find that it consumes increasingly large proportions of their time and energy. 'Free time' is made extremely valuable because of its rarity. In this context, the traditional responsibilities of church membership come as one more demand among the many others. Some respond with resentful compliance, others by opting out completely.

INTRODUCTION: SICK TO DEATH

Church culture has been based on voluntarism. Rightly or wrongly, church programmes have been dependent on people willing to give time, energy and money. The mainstay of this approach has been spouses not in employment. Today economic conditions mean that families can hardly exist on one income. With both partners in a marriage working, home life becomes a complex scheduling of responsibilities and resources, leaving little to contribute to the church.

Some have left because of life experiences which have produced alienation from their faith communities. They include those struggling through divorce, experiencing doubt about their faith, making sense of their own sexual orientation, or even simply coping with a life-threatening illness such as cancer. The problem is not that they are overtly excluded from the congregation. More often it is a case that they find no home among the people of faith in the midst of their crisis. Reactions range from embarrassment to condemnation to isolation. Finding themselves abandoned in their hour of need, such people move reluctantly to the fringes of the congregation. From there it is a short step to the outside world.

All of these circumstances, while reasonable indicators as to why people are leaving the church, are not sufficient in themselves. Rather they point to more serious flaws in the life and practice of the ecclesiastical institution. It is necessary to look below the surface of the church and enquire why it is failing so spectacularly to capture the passions and allegiances of its former adherents.

INTERNAL CONFUSION

Partly as a result of a diminished following, the church in the West has been forced to cope with a number of internal stresses. There is difficulty in recruiting candidates for ministry, particularly for traditions such as Catholicism where a high level of commitment is required. Retaining clergy is an even greater problem. Whether through dissatisfaction, moral failure, or simply impatience with the demands made upon them, leaders of congregations are resigning in large numbers.

One of the causes of the internal strife is the loss of status of the church.[4] There was a time when not only the church was held in high regard, but also the profession of ministry. To be ordained was to be somebody; to have a certain degree of standing and respect by virtue of one's vocation. This is no longer true. Henri Nouwen relates an incident which illustrates the state of ministry:

A few years ago, when I was chaplain of the Holland–America line, I was standing on the bridge of a huge Dutch ocean liner which was trying to find its way through a thick fog into the port of Rotterdam. The fog was so thick, in fact, that the steersman could not even see the bow of the ship. The captain, carefully listening to a radar station operator who was explaining his position between other ships, walked nervously up and down the bridge and shouted his orders to the steersman. When he suddenly stumbled over me, he blurted out: 'God damn it, Father, get out of my way.' But when I was ready to run away, filled with feelings of incompetence and guilt, he came back and said: 'Why don't you just stay around. This might be the only time I really need you.'

Comments Nouwen:

There was a time, not too long ago, when we felt like captains running our own ships with a great sense of power and self-confidence. Now we are standing in the way. That is our lonely position: We are powerless, on the side, liked maybe by a few crew members who swab the decks and goof off to drink a beer with us, but not taken very seriously when the weather is fine.[5]

Clergy have adopted various responses and defence mechanisms in such a climate of disdain. Almost all struggle with a sense of identity and value. A favoured response among Protestants has been to search for an alternative professional model to inform their work; one which retains elements of status and respect.[6] Thus we have seen the rise of the pastor-administrator, who applies the techniques of management to the job. An alternative role is that of pastoral counsellor, in which the minister becomes a therapist to the flock. Still others immerse themselves in the social services, identifying as members of the helping professions. And a final response is to drop out; to adopt a new form of employment which does not result in ridicule.

Ethical failure among clergy has reached epidemic proportions. There is no section of the Christian church in the West which is not dealing with episodes of church leaders crossing sexual boundaries. The level of abuse in such transgressions is high, given the position of trust and responsibility which clergy hold in regard to their flock. It has a similar degree of psychological and emotional trauma to that of a parent abusing their children. The deeply disturbing element is how someone who takes the role of a representative of Christ could end up in such a massive violation of their responsibility.

The difficulties in the ethical area are not limited to clergy, nor to sexual misdemeanours. Christians generally are in a great deal of moral confusion. In the arena of public affairs there are complex decisions to be made. Doctors agonize over their role in abortion, euthanasia or genetic manipulation. Managers face difficult choices in regard to redundancy, or profit-making ventures of marginal legality. Politicians struggle to know how to balance public good with their own dependence on political support. In all of these dilemmas the protagonists are desperately in need of guidance, and may find little help in the church.

Underlying the state of unrest and dis-ease in the church is the collapse of plausibility structures for Christianity. There is the sense among Westerners that Christianity lies in the past of the culture.[7] It is regarded as a stage, like pre-modernism or modernism, that can be happily discarded now that it has served its purpose. Many frustrated Christians encounter this resistance, with little understanding of its source. It is psychologically difficult to maintain specific claims to truth when supporting plausibility structures do not exist.

Some Christians have adopted a survival strategy which involves living a dualistic life. In an unconscious parallel to the Lutheran 'two-kingdom theory', they keep their Christian lives and public lives entirely separate. Different standards for evaluating truthfulness or making ethical decisions operate in the two realms. The world of 'church' becomes an arena in which there is a suspension of the cynicism and scepticism which is necessary in the more public aspects of pluralistic urban life. As Lesslie Newbigin has pointed out,[8] this leads to a crippling privatization of faith, and eventually to the collapse of Christianity in its historical form. Dualism has never been a viable option for a faith-tradition which is strongly universal and world-affirming.

The end result of the collapse of plausibility structures for Christianity is the practical consignment of the religion to the rubbish heap of historical forces which have passed their use-by date. The sudden and almost total demise of Marxism in recent years stands as a warning beacon to those who believe that institutional structure and historical impetus will preserve movements indefinitely. The frightening reality is the extent to which Christianity in the West has already been disposed of in the popular mind as an archaic and oppressive system.[9]

CULTURAL ISOLATION

For all the problems of Christendom (and there were many), it at least represented an era in which the church of Christ had relevance for the broad stream of humanity. The history of Western art bears witness to the deep penetration of the Christian story into the cultural imagination of society as a whole.[10] It is entirely understandable and perhaps inevitable that the new era of pluralism should diminish the centrality of Christian motifs. However, it is less certain that the church should so readily accept its exile to the wasteland of personal religious choices. It is almost as if in the face of new players who will not accept its authority nor its rules, the church has decided to take its game off into a corner where it may continue in peace.

This mentality can result in seeing outsiders as threatening and infectious, and therefore to be shunned. A theological wedge is driven between 'Christian' experience and 'human' experience. It is as if the church has found itself on an ice floe which has broken loose from the polar icecap, only to discover that the floe itself is steadily shrinking. In response the survivors are forced to huddle closer together, and define themselves in distinction from their compatriots who continue to go about their lives on the distant mainland.

Because religious movements attempt to provide ultimate meanings for human experience, they are in serious trouble when they become alienated from that experience. Of course Christians are as human as anyone else, and their experience is by definition human experience. But non-participation in the parent culture of a society quickly begins to warp perception, and limits the ability of the separated group to speak with any insight. The pressing difficulty for the communication of faith in present times is the lack of common ground with the intended audience. As will be argued below, this has little to do with a lack of interest in the central questions addressed by Christianity, and everything to do with the perception that the church has no authentic involvement in the vital issues.

A charge which has been laid at the church's door with regularity and increasing intensity is that of hypocrisy. It is one easily dismissed by Christians as a misunderstanding. But its very persistence may call for a deeper examination. What are people saying when they accuse the church of hypocrisy? In essence the complaint is a reaction against Christians claiming to be better than anyone else. That this is not so is evidenced by the moral failures of Christians outlined above, and received with some glee by outside observers. I believe that such public humiliation is welcomed as the come-uppance of a group which demonstrates a 'holier-than-thou' attitude. Christians are regarded as having placed themselves apart from and above 'ordinary people', and this produces a lingering resentment.

Whatever theological justifications may be offered for the church's demeanour, the fact remains that it is perceived as smugness by the world at large. Christians are not regarded as participants on an equal footing with other members of society, but as a privileged elite who cushion themselves from reality with an insincere piety. The recognition of genuine goodness and compassion requires that the bearers of it are sharing the common struggles of human life, and not separated off into a corner where they can make judgements on others from a place of safety. It is precisely this sense of solidarity in the human endeavour which is missed by those who might otherwise seek some hope in the church.

It seems that the impetus of the incarnation has been lost somewhere in the historical development of the church. Instead of being made present in human life, the God of the church has become remote and thus irrelevant. Christianity in the West is seen as a legitimate religious option for those who are into it, but having no bearing on the broad movement of culture or human evolution.

SPIRITUAL ARIDITY

Whatever the church's problems may be, they do not stem from a lack of interest in God or spiritual development among participants in Western culture. The late twentieth century has witnessed an explosion of interest in spirituality. John Drane comments:

> Rapidly increasing numbers are finding it possible to believe in reincarnation, spirit guides, and extra-terres-

trials, and all sorts of other esoteric ideas. To traditional Christians, this might be unfamiliar territory. But it certainly means that these people are spiritually open as no other generation within living memory has been.[11]

As the modernist matrix disintegrates, people are turning to deeper and supra-rational sources to provide meaning for their lives. The most enthusiastic participants in this quest envisage the current period of history as a flowering of spiritual evolution.[12]

Unfortunately the great majority of these spiritual explorers do not make any connection between their personal quest and the existence of the church.[13] To them, the contemporary Christian church is a relic of a bygone era; a monument to religious sentiment in the past, but irrelevant to the vital pilgrimage they are embarked upon. Those expressions of spirituality which are demonstrated by the church are regarded as shallow and repressive. Christian people seem to them to be materialistic and emotionally stunted. They further appear dogmatic, rigid, and unwilling to experiment spiritually or to learn from experience.

By contrast, many so-called 'New Age' endeavours appear open, exciting, inspiring, adventurous and enriching. There is a sense that the participants are *spiritually alive*, and that their explorations of the spiritual realm are the most important thing in life for them. The Western church suffers by comparison. Worship is often routine and cerebral, even in the Charismatic churches. Truth tends to be presented as propositional, and fixed immutably by the canon of Scripture. Personal growth seems actively discouraged in some traditions, especially if it conflicts with the teaching of the church. Most damning of all, Christians are regarded as dull people who are lacking in spiritual depth.

The harsh truth is that the Western church is in danger of becoming spiritually bankrupt. Spiritual disciplines such as prayer, meditation, fasting and *imitatio Christi* are more talked about than practised. The mystics and spiritual writers of the church are neither read nor understood. Many churchgoers are puzzled by the very notion of spirituality, other than the possibility that it may have something to do with 'faith in Jesus'. It is not surprising that sincere people with a sense of spiritual hunger may turn elsewhere than the church to find something which satisfies.

THE FAILURE OF MISSION

The nineteenth century, under the inspiration of William Carey, is often regarded as the great century of mission.[14] In retrospect, it should perhaps be regarded as the great transplanting of Christianity. While continuing to flourish in the fertile cultural fields to which the faith was exported, Christianity has steadily diminished in those lands which were the 'sending nations'.[15] David Barrett notes that the mushrooming growth of Christianity in the Third World is more than offset by the losses in the Western church.[16] Despite large gains by the Evangelical and Pentecostal sections of the church in the twentieth century; despite endless decades of evangelism; despite the success of Billy Graham; still the church in the West has been steadily retreating.

To be sure, there has been much writing and reflection on mission. Enculturation, people movements, development, syncretism, contextualization; all these have become familiar subjects of theological investigation in relation to foreign mission. Unfortunately, few of the resulting insights have had much impact on the home base. The one massive gap in the church's expertise is *how to do mission in the post-Christian West*. Our churches are structured for preservation and continuity, not for mission.

It is difficult for the church to be in both mission-mode and survival-mode at the same time. A missionary church needs to be open, flexible, reflective, experimental, dynamic and energetic. In order to survive in difficult times, on the other hand, a church will adopt practices which are conservative, exclusive, orthodox, static, careful and scrupu-

12

lous. That is how institutions survive. Unfortunately, it is also how movements die. It is the contention of this book that the church must resist its inherent tendency to conservatism at this critical juncture in its history.

If Emil Brunner is right, then 'the church exists by mission, just as fire exists by burning'.[17] In other words, the church does violence to its own identity as the church of Christ whenever it ceases to express its missionary nature. Mission is not an optional extra for the church.[18] The church needs the continual renewal which is provided by mission, if it is to maintain its authenticity. A pond quickly becomes stagnant when there is no fresh tributary to ensure its sweetness.[19] Unfortunately, for much of the twentieth century, the Western church has wrongly assumed that its mission responsibilities were confined to distant lands. This false security engendered by centuries of Christendom has led to neglect of home-base mission. The result is a dying church.

In former times, the predominant position of the church as a social force meant that citizens of the society confronted the Christ-story by virtue of their participation in the civic community. In such a setting, the church did not feel the need to adopt missiological strategies to bridge cultural divides. There were none. But this era has well and truly gone. The church in the West is isolated and alienated from its host culture. All the old privileges of status, authority and cultural penetration no longer exist.[20] For the first time in many centuries, the Western church has woken up to find itself a small minority in a disinterested and occasionally hostile neo-pagan context. In this setting, missionary orientation is the sole alternative to a lingering death.

Where To From Here?

As a participant in the church, it is easy to be critical; perhaps even harsh. While my description of the woes of the Western church may be perceived as negative, I think it is honest and realistic. We do ourselves no service if we deny terminal illness. I have lost count of the number of revivalist movements which have swept through my homeland promising a massive influx to the church in their wake. A year after they have faded, the plight of the Christian community seems largely unchanged, apart from a few more who have grown cynical through the abuse of their goodwill, energy and money.

It is time for a sober and honest assessment of what is happening. It is time to grieve for the inadequacy of the church of Christ in the Western world. Out of that grief there may come hope. When people relinquish neurotic interpretations of their behaviour and face the cold truth, they become capable of change. Until then they are impotent. Likewise the church remains shackled until it dispenses with comforting illusions:

> For you say, 'I am rich, I have prospered, and I need nothing.' You do not realize that you are wretched, pitiable, poor, blind, and naked. (Revelation 3.17)

The Western church at the end of the second millennium stands in need of comprehensive reformation, if it is to be once again true to its calling.

There is a scriptural story which becomes increasingly insightful, given the current historical crisis of the people of God. It concerns the Israelites and their pilgrimage toward the promised land, following their release from captivity in Egypt. In Numbers 13 and 14, there is the account of their arrival at the frontier of Canaan. They choose spies, and send them out to investigate this strange land, while the bulk of the people remain camped on the other side of the border. When the spies return, they have differing accounts. The majority opinion is that the territory is unsuitable and threatening, being occupied by people of giant stature (Numbers 13.31–3). Caleb and Joshua disagree. They de-

14

scribe it as a 'rich and fertile land', which will be easily conquered with the Lord's help (Numbers 14.5–9).

But the people don't want a bar of it. They feel that their very survival is under threat from the looming confrontation, and begin to long for what they had left behind:

Why is the Lord bringing us into this land to fall by the sword? Our wives and our little ones will become booty; would it not be better for us to go back to Egypt? (Numbers 14.3)

The result of this dispute is that the Israelites back off from the borders of the new land. Caleb and Joshua recognized that even though elements of it were threatening, this territory was indeed the promised land which God had been leading them to. But the conservatism and concern for safety of the majority leads them to retreat. They end up spending another forty years wandering in the wilderness until they come back to the same border again, and find the courage to cross it.

Today the Western church stands poised at the fringes of radically new terrain, albeit historical rather than geographical. Many are frightened by what they see; concerned for their safety and the preservation of the community. There is a deep-seated longing to go back to what we had before. I fear that the majority of Christians in the West are of a mind to withdraw and regroup. Reading the story of the spies, I firmly believe that, now as then, faithfulness requires the crossing of the border. The truth is that there is no way back, and there never has been. The call of God is upon the Western church to take courage and move forward. As ever, the guarantee is not that of safety, but of the continued presence of the nomad God.

Time and again, as I have pondered the way forward, I have been led back to a missionary episode in the life of the early church. It is the story of the encounter between Peter and Cornelius in Acts 10, commonly regarded as the beginning of the mission to the gentiles. The simple narrative of events surrounding this meeting is startlingly radical. It encapsulates the struggle of a faithful follower of Christ to make sense of a new situation; to stay faithful when all the old certainties seem to be stripped away. To a large extent, this book is an extended commentary on Acts 10.1–11.18. I believe this passage of Scripture may provide inspiration and encouragement as we seek to follow Christ in the tension between faithfulness and relevance.[21]

1
Acts 10 – Outside the Box

The book of Acts is the great text of mission. In this Lucan compilation of oral history, we hear the stories of how a localized Jewish sectarian movement became spread throughout the known world.[1] We travel with the embryonic church as it stumbles toward recognition of the significance of this man Jesus, who had caused a minor stir in Palestine. Alongside the pioneers of Christian faith, we learn that the intentions of God in Christ are much wider and more deeply significant than had at first been recognized.

Acts is also a text of the Spirit.[2] From the dynamic epiphany at Pentecost, the first followers of Jesus are time and again astonished as they encounter the work of the Spirit. In times past they had bumbled their way to understanding as they followed the radical prophet, Jesus. Now, still struggling to make sense of the resurrection, they receive rough insights as they are led and confronted by the Spirit. This is of course what Jesus had promised, in the time which suddenly seems so long ago. That he would send someone to lead them into truth. Perhaps they had contemplated something a little less dramatic.

It is in encounters with the Holy Spirit that the early church works out its purpose. Theology is forged in the white heat of experience, where the apostles are moved or challenged or dumbfounded by the Spirit of the living God.[3] If they become missionary apostles, it is only because God does not give them much choice. There are people falling down dead, being blinded, having visions and rising from death or disaster all about them. These great trailblazers who have become role models for us were not so much initiators as responders. They went where God took them, and often observed while God did unthinkable things in their presence.

17

This is an important reminder to us all that the mission is God's. The redemption of the world is as much God's task as was the creation of it. It is within the great pulsating heart of the Trinity that mission is located, and from there it proceeds. To suggest that God has given the church the task of mission is bordering on the blasphemous. Rather God's missiological adventure proceeds within history, and as many as are willing are invited to share in it. It is an open river which flows where it will, into which we may plunge if we have courage enough. This of course means that we cannot control the course or the depth, and that fact may keep us on the bank in safety. But whether we swim in it or simply admire it, the mission of God proceeds.

The Significance of Acts 10

While the tenth chapter of Acts is one story among many others, it has pivotal significance for not only the book, but the whole self-understanding of the church.[4] This chapter describes the events which were to initiate a whole new era of mission history. In the space of a few days, history and tradition were to be turned on their heads.

Up until this point in the nascent movement, Jesus was evolving in status (for the disciples) from being a prophet to being the long-awaited Messiah. The appellation 'Christ' or 'Messiah' only made sense of course within the confines of Judaism. It was part of their religious expression, as uniquely Jewish as David. There had long been outsiders welcomed into the Jewish faith, but only through cere-monies such as baptism and circumcision, which had the effect of changing not only their belief system but their nationality. The nation of Israel was, after all, the people of God; to join the people of God involved joining the nation. Salvation involved uniting oneself with the historical com-munity of divine election, established by covenant. The distinction between Jews and gentiles was less an ethnic classification than a matter of faith.

The church, if we can call it such at this early stage, was a Jewish sect. Certainly the radicality of Jesus had left its mark on his followers and the way they lived, but they would have quite happily remained in Jerusalem and Judaism, if allowed. Gentiles were free to join; but naturally they had to become circumcised, because to follow Jesus was to become a Jew.[5] In the end, many disciples were forced out of Jerusalem through persecution, made fearfully apparent through the stoning of Stephen, described in Acts 7. If Pentecost was the first great movement of the Spirit, this boot up the backside for the community of Jesus was surely the second. It resulted in the dispersal of believers over a wide geographic area.

However, while the location of their faith may have changed, the essence of it had not. Although many were forced into greater interaction with gentiles, their theology of conversion had not altered. To become a follower of Jesus meant to be circumcised (for the men at least) and to learn the tenets of Judaism.[6] How could anyone acclaim Jesus as Messiah if they didn't understand who the Messiah was? So the continuity of Christian faith with Judaism was at this stage stronger than its discontinuity.

It seems that God had other plans. A radical opening of the community of faith was about to take place. The repercussions would be such that on the eve of the third millennium we are still struggling to comprehend what God is about. The experiences of Peter at Joppa and Caesarea initiated the third great move of the Spirit, changing the community of Christ from a dispersed church into an open church. It is to the credit of first-century Christians that they were able to recognize such a disjunctive development as the work of God.

Parallel Visions

The tenth chapter of the book of Acts opens in Caesarea, a garrison city and the administrative capital of Judaea. Here we meet Cornelius, a man of some substance and character. As a Roman centurion of the Italian cohort, he is of course a gentile; a man outside the household of faith. The text tells us that he was a devout man who respected God, and lived a generous and prayerful life. Already the scene is set for the mystery of God working outside the orthodox religious community.

Cornelius receives an angelic visitation. Angels, in the biblical worldview, are messengers. The interest is not in what the angel looks like, or in what mysterious way it appears, but in the message which is brought from God. Cornelius learns two things. First, that he has been heard by God. His prayer life and its outworking in generosity to the poor have risen 'as a memorial' before God. Secondly, Cornelius is instructed to send his own messengers to one Simon Peter, to be found in the house of a tanner in the seaside town of Joppa. There is no explanation of the purpose of this errand, or its likely consequences. The call, as so often in the Bible, requires either obedience or its alternative.

It may be worth reflecting why it is that God should ask this dog-leg detour of Cornelius. If the man's pragmatic faith has already caught the divine attention, why not grant the gift of the Spirit immediately? Why involve Peter? Surely it is because God likes and chooses to work in partnership with human agents in the task of mission. The story of Jesus must continue to be retold, by word of mouth, as it always is. Related to this, and of greater import, is the recognition that evangelism is a two-way street. It is not simply that Cornelius has something to learn from Peter. Peter has a great deal to learn from his meeting with Cornelius. Those who participate in the mission of God receive and learn at the same time as they give and teach.

Meanwhile, the story continues in Joppa. The day after the vision of Cornelius, Peter, gloriously oblivious to what is about to happen, goes up to the roof of Simon's house to pray. Those who have travelled through the Middle East will know what a delightful place the rooftop is in the distinctive architecture of the region. It is a place of relative quietness and openness to the sweep of the sky. The white-wash walls against the azure sky make the flat housetop a pleasant place to relax, sleep or dine. It is around noon, and Peter, feeling hungry, falls into a trance while he is waiting for food to be prepared.

He sees a great sheet descending from heaven, containing animals of various kinds. In his hunger, he sees the giant knapsack as overflowing with a source of potential sustenance, an interpretation which is confirmed by the accompanying voice. Peter is instructed to rise, kill and eat. That he recognizes this voice as belonging to God is apparent in his subsequent appellation of the speaker as Lord. Thus far we might suspect a thoroughly benign vision. God is perhaps reminding Peter that he, the Lord, is the provider of all needs, both spiritual and material. When Peter grows hungry, God will provide.

Except for one smallish problem. The food which God is offering to Peter is proscribed. It is religiously unacceptable; non-kosher. Peter knows full well that the sort of animals that are offered in the sheet are written off the menu by Scripture itself. Leviticus 11 divides various creatures into the categories of clean and unclean for the purposes of consumption. This classification is conveyed as part of the direct revelation given to the people of Israel through Moses (Leviticus 11.1), so that they may style their lives according to the covenant. Observing the culinary divisions into clean and unclean animals is part of dedication to God, a point spelled out in the text:

> For I am the Lord your God; sanctify yourselves therefore, and be holy, for I am holy. You shall not defile yourselves with any swarming creature that moves on the earth. For I am the Lord who brought you up from the land of Egypt, to be your God; you shall be holy, for I am holy. (Leviticus 11.44, 45)

21

Peter, responding out of the depths of his religious tradition, instinctively refuses to transgress the clear boundaries laid down for him by Scripture. The Torah is God-given, God-breathed. Did not Jesus himself say that 'until heaven and earth pass away, not one letter, not one stroke of a letter, will pass from the law until all is accomplished' (Matthew 5.18)? And now does God call him to transgress the precepts of God?

For Peter, submitting to the voice which he recognizes as that of the Lord places him in transgression of and alienation from that same Lord. In terms of scriptural hermeneutics, this is the equivalent of a small nuclear device. On what basis is Peter to validate whether the immediate experiential voice which he is hearing is that of God or not? To accept the vision as carrying the genuine voice of God is to relativize the entire Judaeo-Christian tradition; to transform what had been a secure rock of interpretation into a quagmire.

Whatever else it does, Peter's vision of Acts 10 drives us in the direction of radical dependence on the living God. Those who may be tempted to retreat to the fallback position of quoting Scripture find themselves in the unwelcome position of refusing the Spirit of God.

Peter's confused reluctance earns a reply from God: 'What God has made clean, you must not call profane' (Acts 10.15). This is as clear a statement as we are likely to get of the sovereignty of God. God retains freedom to speak and act, even if such speech and action seems to contravene human understandings of what is divinely permissible. God retains the right to act in new and different ways, as indeed the messiahship of Jesus demonstrates. The effect is to radically open the future. God is not bound by the history of his dealings with humanity, however deeply they may be enshrined within religious tradition.

Peter remains hesitant, understandably. The vision is repeated three times, with the accompanying voice. Presumably this is to reinforce the message in such a way that Peter cannot hide from it. As yet, he has no understanding of the vision's implications. Probably he is still interpreting it within the context of his hunger. The story tells us that he was 'greatly puzzled' (v. 17). But before he has time to reflect at length upon it, there is a commotion outside. The servants of Cornelius have arrived, and the Spirit confirms to Peter that they have been sent to him. The two visions are about to connect in such a way that the direction of the Christian church will be changed irrevocably.

The Caesarea Blessing

Still in something of a confused state, Peter invites the travellers in and hears their story. Their tale confirms what he has just been told by the Spirit, and so Peter receives them. Although he has been instructed to go with them 'without hesitation' (v. 20), he bids them stay the night. It is not until the next day that they set off for Caesarea, in the company of some other Christians from Joppa. It is a journey of some distance, and another day passes before they arrive at their destination.

Through the activity of the Spirit, Peter has had his peace disturbed. God has broken into his existence first through a disturbing vision which continues to nag, and second by this bunch of gentiles who have lured him out of his home in Joppa. Again, we need to pause for reflection on the divine strategy. Would it not have been simpler for God to instruct Cornelius to go directly to Joppa? It certainly would have saved time. Putting aside any difficulties there may have been for a centurion to travel, there may be some significance in the way the story unfolds. We need to remember that this is a story about mission, and one which may come to act as a sort of paradigm for the whole business of mission.

Participating in the mission of God means leaving our place of security, to travel to the place where others are. This is the heartbeat of the incarnation, the movement of God outwards into the creation to stand with us in Jesus. It is the experience of Peter and Paul and the other pioneers of mission. It is the rediscovery of William Carey and the many thousands who followed. Mission is always in the direction of the other, and away from ourselves.

When Peter and his friends complete their journey and arrive in Caesarea, they are welcomed into the household of Cornelius. This Italian officer has invited his friends and extended family, in anticipation of the man whom God was bringing to him. So excited is Cornelius at the arrival of his guest, that he falls down at Peter's feet to worship him. This is misguided religious practice; idolatry. But it is at least a genuine and heartfelt response to the activity of God in Cornelius' life. It is only to be expected that a gentile will not know the finer points of theology or worship. Peter corrects him but does not reject him; a lesson perhaps for many contemporary Christians who are excessively anxious in their encounters with 'New Age' spirituality.

By this stage, with a day on the road to ponder it, Peter thinks he has understood his vision of the unclean animals. As he explains to the crowd gathered in the house, Peter's own religious tradition prohibits him from having anything much at all to do with gentiles: '. . . it is unlawful for a Jew to associate with or to visit a Gentile' (v. 28).[7] He is somewhat surprised to find himself in a gentile house, and would not be there at all, were it not for the fact that: '. . . God has shown me that I should not call anyone profane or unclean'. This is a legitimate interpretation of what God is leading Peter towards, and is certainly in the right direction. But the depth of its meaning has not yet been exhausted.

Having justified his presence, Peter begins by asking to hear Cornelius' story. He wants to know what God has been doing in this man's life to have brought them to their present encounter. This is another point of significance for mission strategy. There is time and opportunity given for the apparent 'pagan' to tell the story of the very real activity of God in his life. Peter listens before he begins to speak, and when he does speak it is with respect for the integrity of his hearer's faith. 'I truly understand that God shows no partiality,' says Peter, 'but in every nation anyone who fears him and does what is right is acceptable to him' (vv. 34, 35).

He proceeds to preach the gospel. Even by the time that Luke was recording these events, the sermons of the early saints had become formulaic. It is difficult for us, at the other end of two thousand years of Christian history, to hear the gospel in a way which is fresh and free of triteness and morphological captivity. Nevertheless, we can at least note that most of what Peter does is very simple. He tells the story of events which he and others have witnessed. The version we have it in records Peter's sermon as nicely rounded out and complete with an 'appeal' at the end. But the text also seems to indicate that he didn't quite make it to the conclusion of his address.

Something stunning happened which was as unexpected as it was inexplicable. The meeting was interrupted in such a way that it would have been very difficult to put back together again. The Spirit fell on those who listened, and they began speaking in tongues. We are told that those believers who had travelled to Caesarea with Peter were 'astounded', as well they might be. These gentiles were neither circumcised nor baptized, and yet here was the unmistakable evidence of God's inclusion of them. It is important to understand that the 'gift of the Spirit' is the promise which is given to those who are 'in Christ', included in the household of the faith. It is the gift of Christ, for those who are followers of Christ. And now we have these ritually unclean gentiles giving unmistakable evidence that they have been 'baptized' in the Spirit.

Peter and his followers look on in awe as God does something new and unprecedented before their eyes. The covenant of Moses, which has been in place for thousands of years, is being broken open as they watch. Given the Jewish faith perspective, these events are incomprehensible. If Peter had not received his threefold vision, he might have rejected the possibility of what his senses were telling him out of hand. As it was, he recognized the work of God, and understood in at least a preliminary way what God was doing. 'Can anyone withhold the water for baptizing these people', he asks, 'who have received the Holy Spirit just as we have?' (v. 47). It was a rhetorical question, a statement of affirmation that God was present and at work. And so the new disciples, already accepted by God, were baptized into the church.

A Missiological Paradigm for Our Times?

There are many dangers in making the events of Acts 10 into a hermeneutical parable. Like the story of the thief on the cross, Acts 10 is a borderline situation: theology *in extremis*. It refers to an important transitional time, when God was leading the church in an entirely new direction. As such, it can hardly become the rule by which we determine our ordinary exegetical work of interpretation. It would be counter-productive to be always playing the experiential work of the Spirit off against the received tradition. This has been done in many historical and contemporary contexts, and has generally led to chaos and abuse, rather than edification.

However, the movement which brings Acts 10 onto the exegetical horizon is the crisis of the Western church, described in the Introduction. It may be that in situations where the past has become unhelpful and the future is unclear, theology *in extremis* is exactly what is called for. It could be that we are experiencing the death of Western Christianity. But equally, it may have seemed that the persecution of Christians following the stoning of Stephen was the end of the church. It definitely seemed to the first disciples, for a time, that the death of Jesus was the end of his messianic mission. It is just possible that our current crisis is a God-given *kairos* moment; an opportunity and incentive to move in a heretofore unseen direction. If so, the theology and hermeneutics of Acts 10 may be signally relevant.

What then are we to take from this account of God's work

among the gentiles, which may be of relevance for our own situation? Several things, I suspect. The first, and most central to this book, is that we must be prepared to let God do genuinely new things within the history of mission.[8] The fact that we have been the community of Jesus for 2,000 years does not mean that we have exhausted revelation, or understood even yet all that God has done in Christ. As the excellent Baptist hymn has it: 'The Lord has yet more light and truth to break forth from his word.'[9] Sometimes, indeed, as was the case for Peter, it may seem that God is nudging us in directions which are contrary to all that we have understood in Scripture.

The people of God have many times been called upon to go beyond their boundaries. This is not a comfortable experience. When boundaries are crossed, there is much legitimate concern for safety and security. How can we know what is right in untested situations, in genuinely new contexts? The only guide we have is to allow God to re-emphasize certain aspects of our history which may be newly relevant. Acts 10 is, I believe, a paradigm for our times. It is the story of an apostle and a community who were prepared to think and act outside the box. This came from a fundamental understanding that God is not a God who likes to be constrained, and has a habit of bursting boxes with delight. This hour of crisis in the West calls for such thinking outside the box; for a radical dependence on God which will allow him to lead us into the new land ahead.

Related to this, and a constituent part of the Acts 10 paradigm, is the recognition that God is active in the world outside the church. People entirely outside the accepted household of faith have relationships with the same God we worship. Their non-Christian spirituality may be un-orthodox, but it also may be received and honoured by God. This breaks open our conceptions of who should and shouldn't be included within the love of God. Like the Jewish church, we may be pushed beyond our comfort zones in learning how wide the purposes of God are within history. We do not hold a franchise on the love of God, and have no legitimate role in restricting access to it.

Those who adopt such a paradigm of mission will make new discoveries. Like Peter, they may be present at the eruptions of God's Spirit in new places. They may become witnesses of whatever strange and wonderful events accompany such encounters. For them, history will be broken open, and the sense of dull fatedness experienced by much of the Western church will be transformed into excitement and spontaneity. These pioneers have an important responsibility as both explorers and reporters of the work of God. The tales they bring back from beyond the borders will need to be interpreted by the wider community of faith as it fumbles toward the future. Whatever happens, it is my conviction that the Western church will be called upon to do its theology outside the box.

2

The Beckoning God

-

The thesis advanced by this book is that the present era in Western development represents one of those rare hinge-points of history. Such a claim can only be made in awareness of the massive temptation for each generation to declare itself unique, and its own circumstances worthy of special consideration. Eventually, the judgement will be made by history itself; those caught up in its flow do not have the advantage of hindsight. Nevertheless, the prophetic calling of the church requires that we do our best to discern 'the signs of the times'.[1] We seek to locate ourselves within the wider perspective of what God is doing in the world, looking for the hints of the divine within the ambiguity of current events.

The church in the West faces a dramatically new situation.[2] Never before has the church faced a post-Christian culture; one which has known and dismissed Christianity as an option. The Western church is not facing incomprehension or opposition so much as a massive indifference. This should not be a cause for despair, if we recall the work of God in previous historical impasses. Whether the people of God are trapped on the shores of the Red Sea, or wandering in the wastes of Sinai, or taken in exile to a foreign land, or driven by persecution from Jerusalem; anxiety is transformed into discovery and celebration as divine intervention in the human story continues.

Crisis situations call into question the received tradition. Acts 10 offers us a paradigm whereby a seemingly new and unprecedented move of God contradicts all that has gone before. In retrospect, of course, we can see that the inclusion of the gentiles was in keeping with the broad thrust of God's work in Christ. But the retroscope is an instrument not available to pilgrims in the present. The apostles were forced to struggle with their revered tradition in the light of a seemingly contradictory present experience.

Re-examining the tradition is no light matter. There are some provisos which surround it. First, as noted earlier, it is theology *in extremis*, and should be reserved for crisis situations. Second, it must be *responsive*, in that it seeks to discern the signs of the times and the action and intent of God within those times. Third, it should be *radical*, in the sense of reclaiming the roots of the tradition rather than introducing new streams from outside. Fourth, it needs to be done *in partnership*, so that the communal nature of the work of theology is recognized.[3] Fifth, it will be undertaken *creatively* and *constructively* in the sense that its end product is a way forward rather than a wholesale destruction of what has gone before. Within these provisos, it may be that the time has come to begin such a process.

A Story from the Frontier

Perhaps it is time to flesh out the theory with a story. If reinterpreting the tradition is to be responsive, what exactly is the process responding to? The following report comes from John Drane, a missionary and theologian who has been particularly concerned to understand the contemporary culture in which he lives. He and his wife Olive live just five minutes' drive from the scene of what has come to be termed the 'Dunblane Massacre'. His experience of the events is an illustrative tale in relation to the situation faced by the Western church. The following account is based on Drane's published recollection, much of it in his own words.[4]

He was leaving a packed prayer vigil in the town, and made his way to the gates of the school where the tragedy had taken place. Here he found a gang of youths aged about 17–20. Drane recounts:

As I watched, they took from their pockets sixteen nightlights – one for each dead child – and, kneeling on the damp pavement, arranged them in a circle, then one of them said, 'I suppose somebody should say something.' As they wondered how to do it, one of them spotted me, identified me as a minister, and called me over with the words, 'You'll know what to say.' Of course, the reality was quite different. As I stood there, tears streaming down my face, I had no idea what to say, or how to say it. Words had not been especially useful to me, or anyone else, in this crisis. So we stood, holding onto one another for a moment, and then I said a brief prayer. That was the catalyst that enabled them too to start praying.

A question came first: 'What kind of world is this?' Another asked 'Is there any hope?' Someone said 'I wish I could trust God.' 'I'll need to change,' said a fourth one. As he did so, he looked first at me, and then glanced over his shoulder to the police who were on duty. He reached into his pocket and I could see he had a knife. He knelt again by the ring of candles, and quietly said 'I'll not be needing this now,' as he tucked it away under some of the flowers laying nearby. One of the others produced what looked like a piece of cycle chain, and did the same. We stood silently for a moment, and then went our separate ways.

Was God in Dunblane? Of course. How could I have been so foolish to doubt it? This was holy ground, and those youths were meeting God in a profound way. Though they would not have expressed it this way, they were repenting. They were reaching out. They were searching for a better way of living, and they had identified a culturally relevant way of expressing their spirituality. As I made my way home that night, I knew for sure God had broken through my tears in a special way, and the deep peace of God about which I had so often spoken now became a living reality in my own spirit.

But make no mistake, there is also challenge here. Those youths instinctively expressed their spirituality not through words, but through symbols. In recent years I have gradually been moving towards the conclusion that our words are getting in the way of the gospel – that the church is somehow imprisoned in a kind of cognitive captivity which is inhibiting our mission, maybe even keeping Christ on the fringes. What would our evangelization need to look like to break out of that bondage? And what would our churches need to be like to create a space to accept and encourage the growth of the kind of spirituality I met that night on a cold pavement in Dunblane?

This compelling narrative raises a number of issues which will inform our reflection on the Western church. Perhaps most importantly, there is the recognition that God continues to be at work in our world, in the lives of ordinary people who are largely disconnected with the church. But, as Drane notes, it is increasingly outside the ecclesiastical institution that genuine spiritual encounter seems to be taking place.[5] What was going on that night in Dunblane? Did those young people meet with the God of our Lord Jesus Christ? How has the church come to be a barrier to mission instead of a launching pad for it?

In order to address some of these questions, and to begin the painful task of reappropriating our Christian tradition, it is necessary to deal with some preliminary matters.

Naught Changes Thee

Does God change? Those of us who have staked our lives on divine faithfulness would certainly hope not. We take solace in the fact that 'here is no shadow of changing with thee'; that in the ephemeral world of mortal existence, we can be sure that 'Thou changest not ... As Thou hast been Thou forever wilt be.'[6] Jesus Christ is the same 'yesterday, today, and forever' (Hebrews 13.8). The unchangeable nature of God would seem to be a foundational element of Christian faith. But then, how do we account for Peter's experience in Acts 10? Why would an unchanging God call on a disciple to transgress something which had previously been recognized as divine revelation?

However, even beginning to talk about the unchangeable *nature* of God betrays a certain Hellenistic slant to our thinking about God.[7] The church has imported ways of thinking about God which have more to do with Greek philosophy than they do with Scripture. The tendency to think of God in terms of attributes – omnipotent, immutable, omnipresent, etc. – is an abstraction which is misleading at best, and heretical at worst. The defining confession for Christians is that 'God was in Christ' (2 Corinthians 5.19). Or again: 'No one has ever seen God. It is the only Son, who is close to the Father's heart, who has made him known' (John 1.18). All preconceptions of God are refined in the crucible of Jesus Christ and his suffering on the cross.[8] Indeed, if God is truly present in Jesus, then God cannot be immutable and impassable; otherwise the suffering of Christ is untenable.

Neither Jesus, nor the Jewish community before him, speak of God in terms of abstract qualities. The stress throughout is on God as *person*; as *someone* who wishes to be in relationship with humanity. The God of Scripture is intensely personal: often portrayed as moody, capricious, passionate and yearning. To those commentators who complain that this is an anthropomorphic view of God (one constructed from our own human image), the response must be that there are no other options. The Christian view of God is vitally anthropomorphic.[9] Our central image of God is of a man crucified on a cross. When the apostle John declares that 'the Word became flesh and dwelt among us' (John 1.14), he is bearing witness to 'what we have heard, what we have seen with our eyes, what we have looked at and touched with our hands' (1 John 1.1). This is the scandal of God made present in human form.

If we want to speak of God as unchanging in some regard (and I am sure we do), we will be getting off on the wrong foot if we start to speak in the abstract. We may do better to think in our necessarily analogical human terms. It would be possible to speak of someone as 'unchanging', though that would be an unusual word to use of a person. We might rather speak of them as being 'rock-solid' or 'dependable'. In these terms, we would be talking of a person's *character*, which is the only part of them which is likely to achieve any sense of constancy. As far as their body, mind and spirit are concerned, these are in a state of flux; either development or decay. This is perhaps a better understanding of what the Bible refers to as 'faithfulness' and 'steadfast love'.

Only in this way can we make sense of Scripture, which says on the one hand that 'God is not a human being, that he should lie, or a mortal, that he should change his mind' (Numbers 23.19); and yet reports on the other that 'God changed his mind' (Jonah 3.10). Human beings know what it is to form a partnership with someone who is constant, faithful and trustworthy. They also know that such a relationship does not exhaust the mysterious depths of the other person. Even after a lifetime, there are new things to discover. A faithful spouse may act in new and surprising ways, and still not be in any way violating their basic character. This may be a helpful way of appreciating the constancy of God while yet leaving room for new developments.

While God remains faithful and consistent, the history of faith demonstrates a wide range of new developments in the divine relationship to humanity, and in human understanding of God's intentions. We do well to be suspicious of all attempts to control the free action of God by the introduction of conventions which we imagine to be binding on the Godhead. If we learn anything from our forebears, it should be that God must be allowed to be God. Even well-intentioned efforts to limit God are misguided.

Our tradition is marked by instances in which the activity of God in history is initially confusing, and seemingly inconsistent with what has gone before. When the territorial God of Israel allows the people to be carried off into exile, when the Temple is destroyed, when the Messiah turns out to be a crucified rebel and blasphemer, when the despised gentiles are included in the covenant; there is an astonishing disjunction which takes some time to make sense of. On later reflection, the community digs deep into its tradition, and finds that in fact these developments are consistent with their received faith. But in each episode, the people's experience and understanding of God is being enlarged.

Discerning the New

It is apparent, then, that while we can speak of God's constancy, it would be mistaken to imagine that this precludes God from either acting in new ways or demonstrating new aspects of the divine character. The one overarching qualification on this is that if it is to be consistent with Christian revelation, we would expect such novelty to be in keeping with what we know about God through Jesus Christ. That is the only way we can have any hope of recognizing God's new activity. To say this is not much different from saying that we would expect any new move from God to be identifiable by having the fingerprints of God all over it.

But while it may be possible for God to act in new ways, we must also ask whether or not it is likely. If God has acted definitively in Christ, does that not preclude fresh initiatives? Does not the closing of the canon put an end to revelation? To give a theologian's answer: yes and no. We would probably want to say that in Christ the alpha and omega, all of God's intentions in history have been presaged. To have looked into the eyes of the crucified Jesus is to have seen the beginning and end of the human story. On the other hand, after 2,000 years of Christian history, we are still unpacking the significance of what took place in the life, death and resurrection of Jesus.

The first disciples were startled by the resurrection, and assumed that God had 'adopted' their beloved rabbi to be Messiah.[10] Gradually it dawned that he may have been Messiah while ambling through Palestine, and so his teaching gained new significance. Finally they began to comprehend that 'the Word became flesh and lived among us' (John 1.14); that they had encountered God in the flesh. Like a ripple spreading on the surface of a pool, the meaning of the Christ-event continued to expand. In a similar way, it has taken centuries for some implications of the gospel to become apparent to the followers of Christ. We need only mention slavery, apartheid, and the place of women within the human community to illustrate how the potential in Christ has only slowly been appropriated.

Discerning the new is no easy task. It is instructive to look to our recent past, and consider the initial difficulties the established church had in accepting the Charismatic movement. Perhaps the fresh winds of the Spirit which stirred the church of the 1970s were softening the Western community for the massive transition which will be necessary to promote Christ in the new millennium. Now there comes a call which compares to that received by Peter in Acts 10. To leave much of what has become secure and familiar, and to strike out for new territory where all is strange, but in which God is active. The call will not be universally appreciated.

New Wineskins

Let us return to the situation in Dunblane, encountered by John Drane. Here we discover the work of God in surprising forms, at a surprising time, and amongst surprising people. The story has some parallels with Peter's experience in the house of Cornelius. In both cases the Spirit is found to be at work in unexpected contexts. Peter asks 'Can anyone withhold the water for baptizing these people?' (Acts 10.47). In an entirely different era, Drane asks: 'what would our churches need to be like to create a space to accept and encourage the growth of the kind of spirituality I met that night on a cold pavement in Dunblane?'[11] Both questions derive from a similar quest: is the community of Christ open enough to receive those among whom God is working?

In essence, of course, the community of Christ is formed through the work of the Spirit, and thus the question contains a tautology. But at a deeper level, what is being asked is whether the historical form of the community of faith is flexible enough to respond to the work of God. At times there is enough correspondence between the two for a vital functional relationship to exist. But we would not be honest if we did not admit that the church often struggles to become what in essence it is, and in certain circumstances may even become unworthy of its name.

The problem is that the community formed by the Spirit gathers around itself certain religious and institutional accretions. This tendency and process is probably unavoidable. Without ongoing conscious efforts at reform, however, the encrustations can so mask the work and love of God as to make it unattainable to either participants or outsiders. This seems to be the essence of Jesus' complaint against the religious institution of Judaism, as represented by the Pharisees: 'For you lock people out of the kingdom of heaven. For you do not go in yourselves, and when others are going in, you stop them' (Matthew 23.13). Considerable anger is directed by Jesus against forms of religion which purport to represent God but end up distancing people from him.

The radical and offensive teaching of Jesus, which undercuts all institutionalism, arises in response to the question as to why Jesus and his disciples differ from the traditional practices of Pharisaic Judaism. His response is apposite to our present discussion:

No one tears a piece from a new garment and sews it on an old garment; otherwise the new will be torn, and the piece from the new will not match the old. And no one puts new wine into old wineskins; otherwise the new wine will burst the skins and will be spilled, and the skins will be

37

destroyed. But new wine must be put into fresh wine-skins. And no one after drinking old wine desires new wine, but says, 'The old is good.' (Luke 5.36–9)

This saying, particularly with the addition of the last sentence of the Lucan version, stresses the discontinuity of the new with the old. While commentators point to the inbreaking of the kingdom as the unique context of the teaching, the story remains powerfully subversive of our own religious institutions.

The testimony of John Drane and other pioneers who are working on the fringes of emerging culture in the West is that God is actively working in people's lives, sometimes in dramatic ways. This missioning activity is frequently far outside the sphere of the church, which seems to have concerns enough to keep it occupied in its own corner of the world. The searching question for the house of faith in the West is whether the church is capable of reform. Sufficient evidence is not in hand yet to be able to make a judgement. The transition needing to be made is great; the future is threatening; and as Jesus says, 'no one after drinking old wine desires new wine'.

The Ties that Bind

Change creates anxiety for human beings. In order to cope with it, we need to find enough that is familiar to act as a substratum, while other aspects of our world are rearranged. In these uncertain times, many Christians have clung to the rock of their Christianity to give themselves a foundational still point. In the process, they may have at times mistaken the forms of devotion with the content of it. It is easy for the accoutrements of faith to become central, and for the reality of God to be forgone for the sake of practices which once mediated that reality.

When the trappings of religion take the place of raw encounter with God, then we have fallen into idolatry, the theme which occupies much of the attention of Scripture. In such circumstances, we may be charged with 'holding to the outward form of godliness but denying its power' (2 Timothy 3.5). This is the unique temptation of the community of faith: to confuse the container of the treasure with the treasure itself. Hans Küng speaks of the 'un-nature' of the church, which is always present where the church exists.[12] In some ways it is easier to be genuinely spiritual outside the church than inside it. Once incorporated as a member, the full weight of institutional pressure is felt, and the radicality of the gospel becomes threatening rather than liberating. This is one reason why the church must continually be refreshed by the influx of new converts.

The elements which constrict us in the pursuit of God are mundane, but no less powerful for that. The forms of our worship, the maintenance of buildings, the misplaced reverence of Scripture, the barrier of group dynamics, the internal politics of the institution, the allegiance to a code of behaviour, the nostalgia for status; all of these can become ties which hobble us. The process of betrayal is subtle and unconscious. Very quickly we find ourselves defenders of dubious territory.

It is the form of the church in the West which has become the biggest barrier to the gospel. The broad sweep of our ecclesiastical life does not bear witness to the grace, passion, radicality, authority, tenderness, anger, excitement, involvement or acceptance of Jesus. Unfortunately for us, the medium has become the message. The popular image of Christianity is formed by encounter with the church; and so Christianity is regarded as reactionary, oppressive, conservative, moralistic, hypocritical, boring, formal and judgemental.

In such circumstances we do well to grieve. Not for what others have done to the church of Christ, but what we, the supposed disciples, have allowed to happen. We are in danger of being counted brothers of Judas; betrayers of Jesus at the same time as we sit at his table. Only by confessing our shortcomings can the hope of change arise within us. This is no time to become protective of the diminishing domain in which we hold sway; rather it is a time to explore uncharted territory, with many dangers and only the promise of Christ to lead us.

To Destroy and to Plant

The ministry of the prophet Jeremiah comes at a critical juncture in the history of Israel. He is to preside over the exile; a time when the Temple and much of the theological certainty which it represented was to be destroyed by the Babylonians. It was not a good time to be a prophet, facing the anger and misunderstanding of a people who felt that God had abandoned them. In Jeremiah's call, his particular vocation is spelled out:

See, today I appoint you over nations and over kingdoms,
to pluck up and to pull down,
to destroy and to overthrow,
to build and to plant.

(Jeremiah 1.10)

Jeremiah's role is to be both *critical* and *constructive*. This seems an appropriate strategy in an era such as our own.

If the church is to be recalled to faithfulness in mission, it must first be honest regarding its own failure. The critical task is necessary and painful. Most of us like neither pain nor grief. We are impatient with it, wanting to skip on to the next step. But when things have gone wrong, then there is no alternative to the hard work of grief.[13] The collapse of the Western church calls for a searching and critical look at our allegiances and representation of faith. Like a patient with cancer, we face the alternative of the incisive pain of surgery or the numbness of death.

The critical task is essential, and the ensuing material will not shrink from it. However, the building and the planting is just as necessary as the plucking up and pulling down. It is

40

too easy to create a wasteland by demolishing the church, without offering any way ahead. The biblical outlook is one of hope and promise; the prophets contrast the deficiencies of the present against the vision of how things might yet be. Their clearing of the ground is the work of the builder in preparation for construction, or the farmer in preparation for cultivation. The true prophetic task is enabling rather than inhibiting, just as the task of the surgeon is healing rather than cutting.[14]

This book will have failed in its task if it does not point beyond itself to the work of God in the world, and the very real hope of the church to continue working in partnership with the kingdom. Here on the border of the third millennium, it is a time of opportunity and promise for the community of Christ. Such promise will not keep us from self-examination and self-criticism, however. We must look full in the mirror and not flinch. Critique and creativity belong next to each other.

Between Caesarea and Dunblane

The next stage of our investigation leads us to examine some of the barriers which church life creates for mission. Some of the elements considered are worthy enough in themselves, but have come to play a restrictive role in the way they are interpreted. There was nothing inherently wrong with circumcision, but at Caesarea Peter realized that this central rite of Judaism was to be placed in proper perspective in relation to the outpouring of God's love in Christ. So it is with topics such as Scripture, holiness and conversion, which will be treated in coming chapters. The crisis of the Western church summons us to re-examine even our deepest certainties.

3

The Bible and Beyond

—

The Bible has a place of special reverence, particularly within Evangelical Protestantism. Frequently referred to as 'the Word of God', the Bible has become the touchstone of orthodox faith and practice for millions of believers. Without papal authority or apostolic succession to rely on, Protestants have placed substantial weight on the foundation of Scripture. A significant portion of any worship service is given over to the reading and interpretation of the Bible. The nature of biblical authority has caused much debate, ranging from serious enquiry into the meaning of inspiration, to the largely semantic but powerfully emotional argument over 'inerrancy'.[1]

For most of those within the church, there is no sense of irony in devoting such attention to a body of literature, the most recent parts of which are some eighteen hundred years old. Christians are 'people of the book', and inescapably so. Our faith is an historical faith, and we are vitally connected to certain events attested to in our scriptures. Without the historical anchor of Scripture, we would be in danger of drifting into the theological stratosphere. Most importantly, the Bible contains the Gospels, which are as close as we can get to eyewitness accounts of the life, death and resurrection of Jesus the Christ. This, for us, is the very heart of faith; without Jesus there is no Christianity.

However, like many good things, Scripture is prone to abuse. In much of the Western church, the way Scripture is handled and appropriated is not worthy of its content. It is often used as a blunt instrument with which to convince people of their sinfulness, or as a talisman of wisdom which protects against unknown dangers. Somewhere along the way, something has gone seriously wrong. Somehow the love, grace and passion of Christ is not being recreated by our reading of the Bible. If we are to recover the heart of mission, Scripture must be rediscovered in a life-giving way.

In order to achieve this, it is necessary to consider the nature and place of Scripture within Christianity. We must make some attempt to understand what has gone wrong, and then seek to correct it. Scripture does indeed have regenerative power, but only when it becomes the instrument of the missionary Spirit.

Jesus and Scripture

Judaism existed without written Scripture for much of its life. The culture was oral, and the tradition was passed from generation to generation in that form. It was not until around the tenth century BCE that canonical material began to be set down in writing. Even then, the resultant text witnesses to its long prehistory in oral culture. By and large, the material collected was anything which was thought to be of significance. The Hebrew scriptures are a strange mix of narrative history, liturgy, prophetic proclamation, genealogy, religious prescription and royal succession. Special place is given to *Torah*, or teaching.

This is provided in the context of covenant, in which the faithful pledge of Yahweh toward Israel requires a lived response from the people, as a demonstration of their faithfulness.[2] While Torah is often objectified as the Law, in essence it is a relational commitment from the worshipping community to live according to the way of God. The Torah and other elements of Scripture were the documentation of relationship, rather than the essence of it. A modern analogy might be a pre-nuptial agreement, in which the outer perimeter is established, but which in no way defines the relationship which generates it.

By the time of Jesus, the Hebrew canon was pretty much closed. A central body of literature had been recorded and refined over a long period, and was now accepted as providing a central repository of the faith. One of the forces at work in the establishment of a canon was a concern for the preservation of the faith. When the people were carried off into exile; when the Temple was destroyed; when inter-marriage with other cultures introduced alien religious practices – how was the integrity of the faith to be maintained? Increasingly, attention shifted to Scripture as a guarantee of continuity and orthodoxy. The Hebrew scriptures were seen as constitutive of the people, and so came to have a revered place in religious life.[3]

With many foreign influences at work, and Israel suffering from a long period of conquest and domination by other powers, preservation of the faith became paramount. In particular, devotion to the law became a test of faithfulness. In what was regarded as a hostile climate, religious leaders looked for external indicators of piety. The Pharisees, in particular, were concerned to keep alive the faith in its purity.[4] They, along with others in the community, yearned for the coming of the Messiah who would overthrow Israel's enemies and restore self-determination to the people. They fervently believed that only when the law was kept would the Messiah come.[5] And so they devoted themselves to observation of not only the Torah, but any extra protective measures which would help to keep it in place.[6]

This is the context into which Jesus comes. Much has been written about the relationship of Jesus to Scripture. Perhaps the majority of comment has pointed to his continuity with and fulfilment of Scripture.[7] Attention has focused on the Matthean version of the Sermon on the Mount, and particularly the interpretive explanation given in Matthew 5.17–20, where Jesus assures his hearers: 'Do not think I have come to abolish the law or the prophets; I have come not to abolish but to fulfil' (v. 17). However, the sort of fulfilment which Jesus proceeds to enact is so radical that it strikes his contemporaries as debasing and contradicting Scripture. Eventually it leads to his execution as a blasphemer.[8]

What are the elements of Jesus' teaching and behaviour which lead to this analysis? He heals people on the sabbath

(Mark 3.1–6). He cuts across family obligations which are clearly set out in the law (Luke 9.59–62). When his own family makes claims upon him, he is dismissive (Mark 3.31–5). In defiance of accepted tradition, he supports his disciples when they gather grain on the sabbath (Matthew 12.1–8). Jesus mixes among, eats with, and takes it upon himself to forgive clearly identifiable sinners (Luke 7.36–50). Most shockingly of all, he undercuts the whole Jewish religious categorization of clean and unclean, which is deeply rooted in the Torah (Luke 11.37–41). This is scriptural subversion in the extreme: 'Thus the demand of Jesus was wholly new and unexpected for it required an allegiance which went counter to the requirements of the Law, struck at the highest social custom of the day, and ran the risk of complete misunderstanding.'[9]

On what basis can such prima facie contradiction of the Jewish law be interpreted as fulfilment? It is not surprising that many good church-going people of the time saw Jesus' nod in the direction of Scripture as prevarication. In the face of determined opposition, Jesus presents his own defence by the judicious use of provocative questions and responses. 'Is it lawful to do good or to do harm on the sabbath, to save life or to kill?' (Mark 3.4). 'The sabbath was made for humankind, and not humankind for the sabbath' (Mark 2.27). 'Go and learn what this means, "I desire mercy, not sacrifice." For I have come to call not the righteous but sinners' (Matthew 9.13). 'First clean the inside of the cup, so that the outside also may become clean' (Matthew 23.26).

It is worthwhile noting the strategy which Jesus is adopting in his retorts to accusers. He respects Scripture, often quoting it to substantiate a point. But more importantly, he drives down into the heart of the tradition, in order to bring out what lies behind it. Such an approach is neither *liberal* (in terms of hanging loose from Scripture), nor *conservative* (by way of justifying current religious practice through the use of Scripture). Rather it is *radical*, in that it seeks to return to the roots of the tradition, and to draw attention to the intent of God concerning humanity.

He confounds his critics by appealing to the same sources as them, but arriving at an entirely different practice.[10]

This is the true value of Scripture. It may only be the outward trappings of living faith, but it provides a means of access to the heart of the faith. However corrupt or misguided the religious community may become, as long as it carries Scripture within its womb, it carries the subversive seeds of its own overthrow. Jesus does not dismiss what has gone before, but from it uncovers the heart of God. In his hands, Scripture is transformed from being regulatory, restrictive and objective, to being generative, reforming and life-giving.

On Tablets of Human Hearts

When people are in love and intend to devote themselves to each other on a long-term basis, it is common to have a ceremony to make public the intention. Marriage is a recognition that rights and responsibilities have changed for the two people who previously went about their own affairs pretty much as they wanted. From that point on, it is accepted by society that the pair are bound together not only emotionally, but legally, morally and historically. They have covenanted to spend their life together, and absolute freedom is curtailed for both parties (with their agreement) by virtue of their relationship. The story of Israel is the story of just such a covenanting together between God and a people.

The ten commandments, and the wider law which they headline, are but the marriage agreement between Israel and Yahweh. It is a move toward relationship on the part of God: 'Now therefore, if you obey my voice and keep my covenant, you shall be my treasured possession out of all the peoples. Indeed, the whole earth is mine, but you shall be for me a priestly kingdom and a holy nation' (Exodus 19.5, 6). Even at this early stage, the commitment to Israel is seen as one of function in relation to God's wider concern for 'the whole earth'. Within the context of the covenant, the law functions as a sort of guidebook for married behaviour.

Moses comes down from Mount Sinai with the tablets of stone, a tangible sign of the sealed relationship, akin to a wedding ring. They are to be kept and treasured by Israel, eventually finding a home in the appropriately named 'ark of the covenant'. As with many marriages, things do not always run smoothly. Yahweh finds that his people are not satisfied with the confines of the covenant, and that they seek satisfaction outside of their relationship. The most poetic expression of this comes in the divine revelation through the prophet Hosea:

> Plead with your mother, plead –
> for she is not my wife,
> and I am not her husband –
> that she put away her whoring from her face,
> and her adultery from between her breasts, . . .
>
> For their mother has played the whore;
> she who conceived them has acted shamefully.
> For she said, 'I will go after my lovers;
> they give me my bread and my water,
> my wool and my flax, my oil and my drink.'
>
> (Hosea 2.2, 5)

It is apparent that the covenant, and the law which enshrines it, is being continually flouted by the human side of the partnership. God is tempted to give up on the relationship altogether:

> What shall I do with you, O Ephraim?
> What shall I do with you, O Judah?
> Your love is like a morning cloud,
> like the dew that goes away early.
>
> (Hosea 6.4)

The people have objectified their relationship with God, and imagine that somehow their participation in the religious rituals will suffice. They are missing the point entirely:

> For I desire steadfast love and not sacrifice,
> the knowledge of God rather than burnt offerings.
> (Hosea 6.6)

So it is that God determines to take a new approach to dealing with the people he desires. The formal agreement seems not to have been successful, succeeding only in driving a wedge between the actions of people and the motivation which lies behind them. A new way of forming a relationship, which may allow for genuine passion and faithfulness, is presaged:

> The days are surely coming, says the Lord, when I will make a new covenant with the house of Israel and the house of Judah. It will not be like the covenant that I made with their ancestors when I took them by the hand to bring them out of the land of Egypt – a covenant that they broke, though I was their husband, says the Lord. But this is the covenant that I will make with the house of Israel after those days, says the Lord: I will put my law within them, and I will write it on their hearts; and I will be their God, and they shall be my people. (Jeremiah 31.31–3)

The theological effect of this shift is to take the emphasis on the external manifestations of religious behaviour, and shift it firmly into the arena of love, relationship, conscience and responsiveness: the arena of the heart.[11] It is this shift from outward obedience to inner relationship which characterizes the ministry of Jesus. His complaint against the Pharisees is that they have put the law and its requirements in the place of God, and assumed that their fulfilment of it was all that God required:

For you are like whitewashed tombs, which on the outside look beautiful, but inside they are full of the bones of the dead and all kinds of filth. So you also on the outside look righteous to others, but inside you are full of hypocrisy and lawlessness. (Matthew 23.27, 28)

The institution of the new covenant is of course the work of Jesus. In his death and resurrection he institutes and allows a new means of relationship to God: 'This cup that is poured out for you is the new covenant in my blood' (Luke 22.20). Consequently, and with the gift of the Spirit to guide human hearts, a better and more intimate relationship has been established between God and creation: 'For God has done what the law, weakened by the flesh, could not do' (Romans 8.3). In the new environment, Paul is able to say of believers: 'you are a letter of Christ, prepared by us, written not with ink but with the Spirit of the living God, not on tablets of stone but on tablets of human hearts' (2 Corinthians 3.3). What the law and the Scripture which contains it have been impotent to do, Christ has achieved through making a direct channel between God and the human heart.

Faith vs Religion

As Karl Barth has unforgettably reminded us, Christian faith is something quite different from religion.[12] Yet religious longings can easily contaminate Christianity. Our fundamental fear of God, and the demands which involvement may bring, are responsible for our (mostly unconscious) desire to filter the raw experience of God. We are constantly tempted to introduce some intermediaries into the relationship, and get God back on the outside where a little more objectivity is possible. The filters can take many subtle forms; for Christians the greatest hazard is that we objectify the outward trappings of faith in order to make life more manageable. Prayer, church attendance, good living, sobriety, giving, clergy and theology can all serve this purpose, given the chance.

The new dynamic and relational covenant may bring more freedom, but sometimes freedom can be a poor substitute for certainty. In the story of The Grand Inquisitor, from Dostoevsky's *The Brothers Karamazov*, Jesus returns to Seville in Spain during the inquisition of the sixteenth century. He is quickly recognized by the Grand Inquisitor, who locks him in prison before he can do any harm. The clerical prosecutor accuses Jesus of presenting humanity with an impossible gift:

> Instead of seizing men's freedom, You gave them even more of it! Have You forgotten that peace, and even death, is more attractive to man than the freedom of choice that derives from the knowledge of good and evil? ... You wanted to gain man's love so that he would follow You of his own free will, fascinated and captivated by You. In place of the clear and rigid ancient law, You made man decide about good and evil for himself, with no other guidance than Your example ... think now, was this the best that You could offer them?[13]

Structure, authority, ritual and control are the religious enemies of Christian faith. The longing for order and security are powerful human forces. They continually seek to reassert themselves within the life of the church.[14] Because of this, the community of Christ finds itself perpetually in need of reformation.

The quest for certainty was only heightened by the relativizing effects of the Enlightenment, and so Protestantism (without papal authority) clung more closely to the Bible for security. While Scripture is worthy of foundational status, the place that it has assumed and the way in which it is used have created real problems. Under the new covenant, the longing for certainty almost always arises from religious longings, and so corrupts all that it touches.

Particularly for Evangelical Protestants, Scripture has come to obscure Christ more than to reveal him, and this is inexcusable.

Bibliolatry

The major concern of Scripture is not atheism, but idolatry. The Bible does not bother to make much of a case for the existence of God, assuming that God is self-evident to an unbiased humanity. It is deeply worried, however, that God be correctly identified, and that people do not give to pretenders that which belongs to God. The first commandment, after all, identifies God and warns, 'you shall have no other gods before me' (Exodus 20.2). No thing and no body is to take the place of God. Creation reveals God, but it is wrong to worship the creation instead of the creator. In precisely the same way, Scripture reveals God, but it is wrong to worship Scripture instead of God. The current attitude to Scripture in Evangelical churches borders on bibliolatry.

The Bible is not the word of God.[15] It may contain the word of God, in the way that a womb may contain a baby. But the womb is not the baby. Scripture may become the word of God under the inspiration of the Spirit, and often does. But it is heretical and idolatrous to imagine that the word of the living God can be objectified in such a way that it exists within and is limited by a set of printed words on a page. The word of God cannot be separated from the relational presence of God.[16] The word of God is the self-communication of God, and therefore is dynamically connected to the person of God. One cannot know the word of God without knowing God.

Furthermore, the self-communication of God finds its highest point in Jesus Christ. The whole weight of the Christian tradition is that 'the Word became flesh and lived among us' (John 1.14). The ultimate revelatory

51

expression of God to humanity is provided in a person, Jesus of Nazareth.[17] Scripture provides us with our best access to his life and teaching. But neither the words of nor the words about Jesus are a substitute for relationship with him.

Some of this Evangelicals would affirm. But in practice, the Bible has taken on a *functional* role within the church as a new law. That is to say, it is often used as a substitute for personal encounter with the living God. It becomes a means of objectifying God and distancing oneself from the threat of divine intimacy. At this level, Scripture is a safer option than relationship. In my experience of Evangelical churches, it is possible for the Bible to assume the place and devotion which is legitimately intended for God alone. In this way, Scripture ceases to point beyond itself, and so becomes the object of idolatry.

The claim that Evangelical use of the Bible conceals Christ is a serious one, and needs some explanation. Recently, a theological student made an emotional statement in the last lecture of a course. He was a thorough Evangelical, having been brought up and immersed in Baptist life and culture. Along the way, he had participated in innumerable Bible studies and listened to interminable sermons. And yet, he confessed to the class, 'I feel as if I hardly know who Jesus is at all.' For the first time, looking at the Bible outside of his church context, he had encountered the hard and strange sayings of Jesus, and begun to feel the radicality of Christ's call upon his life. With some pain he recognized how distant his own life was from what Jesus was on about.

For the first time in his life, this student had broken through the smokescreen of 'biblical teaching', and heard the unmediated voice of Jesus calling to him. The Bible had ceased to be a protective barrier and source of security in his religious longings, and had suddenly become dangerous. After a lifetime of familiarity with the so-called 'word of God', he came face to face with the Word of God in a manner which could not be ignored. He felt somewhat disappointed that the church which he loved had managed to conceal this treasure from him for the whole of his life.

As the Western church faces a critical juncture in its life and mission, its use of Scripture may have become an effective shackle to the gospel. It is not that we must move away from Scripture, but rather that we should restore it to its proper place. God must be allowed to be God, with all the uncertainty and insecurity which that brings for the church. We must learn again how to use Scripture to lead us to God, rather than as a formal guide to good religious behaviour.

The Cerebral Captivity of the Bible

In retrospect, it is easy to see that the Enlightenment caused a great loss of confidence for the Western church. Galileo and Copernicus occasioned the initial cracks in the great reservoir of faith, and the church's attempt to stick its finger in the hole was always doomed to failure. The great flood of scientific exploration burst upon the world, and seemed to sweep faith-claims away as so much flotsam. It has taken until the end of the twentieth century for the waters to subside. In the meantime, the church cast about for rocks to cling to, and discovered Scripture as a place of refuge.

Unfortunately, the approach taken to Scripture was subtly shaped by the tides of the Enlightenment. In deference to the age of science, a scientific methodology was applied to the study of the Bible.[18] This took place at a number of levels, from the historical-critical method adopted by biblical scholars to the expositional style of preaching which defined Evangelicalism. The common feature of these approaches was the objectification of the text as an item for examination. While the preachers might object to this characterization, there is no doubt that Protestantism became obsessed with doctrines and 'scriptural principles'.

As a generalization, the Bible has been treated in Evangelical circles as if it were some sort of textbook, with a unified content. The attempt has been made to isolate 'principles' from among the varied material of Scripture, and thus extract a codified system of beliefs and doctrines by which to structure life and worship.[19] 'Bible study', and to a certain extent preaching, becomes the exercise of recovering these principles from the raw material of Scripture in which they are embedded. The resultant schema is then used as a framework within which to understand all of the Bible. Some bits are clearly more useful than others, and the Pauline epistles have proved a fertile ground for such investigation.

The problem with this attitude to Scripture is that it is almost entirely cerebral. It has arisen within modernity, 'the age of reason', and reflects the historic bias toward the mind as supreme arbiter of reality. Evangelical worship, with its emphasis on expository preaching, is in constant danger of becoming cerebral, linear, verbal, and hopelessly intellectual. While the mind certainly has a place within faith, it is not the dominant position which it has been granted within many churches.

Playing intellectual games through the discussion of doctrine and 'biblical principles' is the royal route to avoidance of confrontation with God. Our rational belief structure is tightly knit, and functions as an impenetrable shield against the wildness of the Spirit. Belief becomes a matter of mental assent, allowing us to go about our business in other areas of life, while resolutely claiming to be 'Bible-believing Christians'. In the same way that the law functioned for later Judaism, Scripture provides us with a no-man's-land between the presence of God and the chasms of our hearts.

Talking about faith is no substitute for living it. The God of Jesus Christ wants more of us than our minds. Jesus' captivating dream of the kingdom of God involves more than a change in philosophical allegiance. If we are to unleash the power of the Spirit in our midst, it will be important to allow Scripture to once again captivate the whole of our humanity, and lead us bleeding and wailing to the very doorstep of God.

The Truth Shall Set You Free

What then is the proper use of Scripture? How are we to avoid the pitfalls of worshipping it, intellectualizing it, or using it as some sort of magical charm? The answer must be that the Bible is the womb which carries the treasure of the gospel. With the Spirit as midwife, Scripture remains capable of giving birth to Christ within us. In a Christian culture where the forces of religion often hold sway, the Bible keeps alive for us 'the dangerous memory of Jesus'. Our Scripture is the repository of stories and associated bits and pieces from generations of people who have tried to follow God. It is also the bearer of the 'story of all stories': the life and teaching of Jesus.

It is the source of truth, certainly; but not the sort of smug intellectual truth which keeps people feeling sure of themselves. Rather it introduces us to the Living Truth, the Word of God, Jesus the Christ. The unavoidable bedrock of biblical faith is that truth is personal. It is an integral part of a personed Godhead, and consequently only known through relationship. The Bible is not a textbook nor a rulebook nor an instruction manual. It is a collection of peripheral material generated by a passionate love affair between God and humanity. Those who do not participate in the affair have no hope of making sense of the associated writings.

God decided to dispense with the objective law as a means of mediating love. Instead, God would write on tablets of human flesh, revealing the divine love in immediate and intimate encounter. The hallmarks of the gospel are love and freedom. When Jesus is asked for the essence of faith, he reduces the whole teaching of Scripture to two commandments:

> 'You shall love the Lord your god with all your heart, and with all your soul, and with all your mind.' This is the greatest and first commandment. And a second is like it: 'You shall love your neighbour as yourself.' On these two

commandments hang all the law and the prophets. (Matthew 22.37–40)

Or to summarize it even further in the words of Augustine: 'Love (God) and do what you like.'[20] The emphasis in the new covenant is not on outward actions at all. It is on love and relationship; the unconditional love of God finding a home and response in our own hearts, and the overflow from this into our relationships with those around us. This is a very fragile and seemingly insubstantial base on which to build the kingdom. Many of us have better ideas, and constantly try to implement them. But the gospel slices through our religious titivations, calling us relentlessly back to the simplicity of relationship with the living God. Without the Bible, religiosity would hold sway; we need Scripture to repeatedly wake us from our deathly dreams.

In order for this to happen, Scripture itself must be set free. We must resist its ownership and use as an instrument of control within the ecclesiastical institution. It will mean breaking the shackles of cerebral captivity, and bringing our hearts, emotions, bodies and lifestyles to Scripture, and through Scripture, to God. The gospels, in particular, need to be set free to do their radical work among us. If we dare to remember that Jesus accepted and forgave sinners, we may begin to believe that there is a place for us as well. We should recapture the oral tradition which lies behind the Bible by hearing and telling the stories again, and allowing them to mix freely with the stories of our own lives.

4

The Weariness of the Church

—

The greatest barrier to the gospel in contemporary Western culture is the church. The forms of the church, its life and pronouncements; these act to prevent people from hearing the liberating story of Jesus. In the early days of the church's expansion through the Roman Empire, the cultural context was not unlike our own. Then, however, the church was regarded as new, fresh, exciting and revolutionary. Now, the church is seen as tired and reactionary.

In a course which I teach on 'Church and Society', I ask the students to interview people who have no connection with the church on their impressions of it. The following are some of the comments which they have collected:

> Boring, irrelevant, a clique, a club like Lions Club. They have their own language and set codes of behaviour, which are unwritten. Places where the format of the gathering is very false, the accepted cultural norm is a surface thing. You're not supposed to ask questions or have problems ... Very narrow outlook on the world. Life is church – introverted, isolated, insular.
>
> Church is for a particular group in society . . . good, well-meaning people who have a different idea of fun than normal people ... a naive and behind-the-times club. Kind of like the 60s-style dance nights; the difference being that the people at the dance have fun.
>
> [Church] is like an old car that the owners are all sentimental about but which doesn't do the job anymore. You can't tell them it's time to replace it. You can only see that when you're not so attached to it.

However hurt Christians may feel about these impressions, the most mature response to them will to be ask how we have allowed the community of Christ to gain such a reputation among onlookers.

In Australasia we use the term 'white-anting'. It derives its meaning from the Australian white ant, which has a fondness for wood fibre. White ants will eat their way through the interior of wooden framing in a building, completely hollowing it out. The surface of the timber seems perfectly intact, and there is no obvious evidence of the ants' activity. No evidence, that is, until the entire building collapses. The Christian church in the West has been 'white-anted'. On the surface it appears intact. But the heart of the church has been eaten away, and the whole edifice stands in danger of imminent collapse.

Christianity has been smothered by churchianity. The guardians of the tradition have become impervious to it. In the book of Revelation, the risen Christ says to the church of Laodicea: 'For you say, "I am rich, I have prospered, and I need nothing." You do not realize that you are wretched, pitiable, poor, blind, and naked' (Revelation 3.17). These are words which sound ominously like a potential epitaph for the Western church. Churchianity, the creed of the religious institution, is a powerfully assimilating movement, and antithetical to the gospel. It is important to understand some of the crippling dynamics of it, if we are to escape its influence.

The Faith of the Middle Class

Syncretism is usually regarded as a problem arising in foreign mission fields. It involves the importation of inappropriate cultural values or customs into the Christian faith. Historically, missionaries have regarded as syncretistic such episodes as national Christians retaining totems to their ancestors, or continuing to consult traditional spiritual healers. For much of Christian history, it was assumed that Western Christianity didn't suffer from syncretism. The Christianity of the missionaries was regarded as

gloriously neutral and free of cultural contamination.
'biblical' or 'orthodox' Christianity. It is only wi
globalization of the faith that this myth has proved 1
able.

Western Christianity, as viewed from those outside of the
culture, is a Trojan horse; occupied by a host of values
which have much to do with cultural perspectives and little
to do with Jesus of Nazareth. It is one of the great benefits of
the current crisis in confidence that we Western Christians
can begin to recognize our own syncretism.

The core beliefs promoted by the church closely resemble
the values of the liberal Western middle class. This is
evident when we examine the church phenomenologically;
interpreting belief in terms of what people do and how they
live, rather than on the basis of what they say they believe.
There is a concurrency of lifestyle among Western Christians which reinforces central middle-class aspirations, such
as consumerism, individualism, careerism and security. The
result is a deeply syncretistic amalgam of Christian language
with a strong cultural perspective. It is what Metz has
described as 'bourgeois Christianity'. We will briefly look
at some of the features of it.

An effective method of analysing Christian belief in the
West is to inspect the car park of a worshipping congregation. Here will be found evidence of the unchecked *consumerism* which marks Christian lifestyle. It is representative
only. A closer inventory could be made, including such
items as home ownership, household appliances, electronic
equipment and wardrobe holdings. The evidence would
reveal that there is very little difference between Christian
attitudes to possessions and that of the surrounding middle
classes, except that Christians pay a voluntary tax to support
the ecclesiastical institution.

There might be no problem with this, were it not for the
teaching of Jesus. He himself had grown up in what might
be described as a middle-class setting. However, he chose to
realign himself, taking on a life of voluntary poverty and
mixing with the riff-raff of his society. Jesus seems to regard

the hunger for wealth and possessions as contradictory to the pursuit of God. He blesses the poor and pronounces woe on the rich (Luke 6.20–6). He warns: 'Be on your guard against all kind of greed; for one's life does not consist in the abundance of possessions' (Luke 12.15). It is easier, says Jesus, for a camel to pass through the eye of a needle than for the rich to enter the kingdom of God (Luke 18.25). He declares that it is not possible to serve both God and wealth (Matthew 6.24).

Jesus' attitudes to wealth and poverty are related to their bearing on *availability*. A life of acquisitiveness, in which the gathering and protection of possessions has a high priority, is incompatible with a life of discipleship and mission. The church is a powerfully socializing entity, in which core values are promoted and reinforced. Because materialism is accepted so unheedingly in the Western church, and is modelled by the majority of mature Christian leaders, it has become normalized as a valid expression of Christian life. Furthermore, like the rich young ruler, many Christians have become enmeshed in a lifestyle of consumption, and are therefore conscious of how much they have to lose in the following of Jesus.

Nor are things much better if we examine the extent of *individualism* in the life of the church. Ever since Descartes made his individual cogitation the arbiter of all truth, Western society has become remarkably individualistic. From its worst expressions in selfish hedonism to the nobler sentiments of the human rights movement, our age is founded on the life, progress and protection of the individual. The destructive elements of this approach to life are currently being felt as our society disintegrates under the pressure of everybody doing what is right in their own eyes. As a philosophy of humanity, individualism is depressingly shallow.

From the nature of the Trinity, from the creation of humanity in partnership, from the divine answer to the question 'Am I my brother's keeper?', the biblical perspective is relational and communitarian. Humanity, participating in the life of God, is created to be in relationship. Jesus works out his mission in the context of community. When he calls disciples to himself, they immediately become part of a group of followers. They are to 'love one another' (John 13.34), 'deny themselves' (Matthew 16.24), and to 'wash one another's feet' (John 13.14). Life in the kingdom is inextricably linked with the welfare of one's neighbour.

And yet our congregations continue to function as conglomerations of committed individuals, little different from a bowling club or a Rotary group. Most Western Christians regard even major life decisions as their private arena, and would never contemplate opening the process to fellow Christians. Similarly, what one does with one's money is nobody else's business. The individualizing and privatization of faith distorts it in a way that distances it from the tradition of Jesus. Christian community, or *koinōnia*, has a potential giftedness about it. It is a mode of existence which makes Christ present to the world in an attractive way. Unfortunately it is hardly ever experienced in the West, because of its cost in terms of commitment.

Individualism and consumerism are strong influences in creating a powerful formative force within the church, which, for want of a better term, may be called *careerism*. This is the belief that one's life is to be evaluated in terms of the work one performs, and that advancement within such work is a mark of God's blessing. This measure is of course widely accepted within the broader community, as a means of establishing a person's worth. It is a peculiarly Western phenomenon, with most other societies opting for genealogy, place of birth or class as the determining characteristics of status.

That the same influence should be promoted within the church is a clear indication of syncretism. Contrary to James' injunction against 'acts of favouritism' (James 2.1), there is a clear grading of occupations within the church. At the top of the tree are the professions: doctors, lawyers, engineers, teachers. These are the people most likely to fill positions of responsibility within the ecclesiastical structure;

also most likely to candidate for ministry. At the bottom are those engaged in menial tasks. The unemployed are often an embarrassment. It is no coincidence that the same grading is to be found within the unwritten charter of the middle classes, whose orientation is always upward.

A preoccupation of the middle classes is for *security*. They are close enough to the lower classes to feel threatened by them, and not wealthy enough to guarantee isolation from all that may go wrong in life. Hence the boom in insurance, superannuation and the 'security industry'. Does the church show any difference in perspective? It would seem not. Jesus says 'Those who want to save their life will lose it, and those who lose their life for my sake, and for the sake of the gospel, will save it' (Mark 8.35). 'Do not worry about tomorrow,' he counsels (Matthew 6.34). 'Make purses for yourselves that do not wear out,' he suggests, 'an unfailing treasure in heaven, where no thief comes near and no moth destroys' (Luke 11.33). But there are few in the West willing to take him at his word.

The Western church has unwittingly become the divine legitimation for the cultural values of the middle class. One benefit of this is that by and large the middle classes have easier entry into the world of the church than some others. In the process, however, the church has departed from the life and teaching of Jesus to such an extent that it has lost both the incisiveness and attractiveness of his radical message. When the church becomes another leisure-time activity for the comfortable, it does not do well in the face of the competition. The faith of the middle class is not necessarily abhorrent; but neither is it the gospel.

Apathy

A common epithet applied to the church in contemporary society is that of 'boring'. It is difficult to imagine this description being used of Jesus, or of the people who followed him through Palestine. Somewhere along the way, a movement which was vital, dangerous and exciting has lost its way, and been domesticated.

Apathy is, literally, the lack of passion. Moltmann has remarked on the sickness of apathy, noting the dual meaning of passion as commitment to life, and suffering.[1] The two are vitally connected. Passionate people are considered dangerous in the ecclesial setting, where moderation reigns supreme. Leaders may be concerned about 'excess' or 'enthusiasm'. Even many of the Pentecostal services, which may have held some legitimate claim to passion at one stage, have evolved into a pattern which has become both familiar and quasi-liturgical. The worshipping community, however, is simply a reflection of the people who participate in it. Somehow the following of Jesus has become less than a life and death affair, and fails to excite the imagination of those who drowse in the pews.

Moltmann writes:

Jesus' life is inspired not just by the wish for a life *after* death, but by the will for life *before* death, yes, even *against* death. Where the sick are healed, lepers are accepted, and sins are not punished but forgiven, there *life* is present. Freed life, redeemed life, divine life is there, in this world, in our times, in the midst of us. Where Jesus is, there is life.[2]

If this be true, then the searching question for the church must remain: Where is Jesus? Are our tired congregations communities of Christ, or have we, like the Pharisees before us, grasped the form and lost the content of red-blooded faith?

A passion transplant will not come without cost. The lurking suspicion is that our dalliance with tedium is the direct result of neglecting discipleship and the price which it bears. The West has sold us the illusion of suffering-free existence. This attempt to exclude pain and suffering from human existence is the besetting sin of Western life. But for the church to participate in this deception is an act of betrayal against the Suffering Servant who has become Lord. Pain is part of life; the attempt to exclude it has the unintended consequence of diminishing the capacity for experiencing life.

In reality, of course, there is no human existence without pain. But in a context where suffering is denied and regarded as failure, then those in the midst of pain are isolated and marginalized. They become a threat to the mythic ideology of pain-free existence, and so their experience must be silenced. Tragically, this has become the fate of many people within the church. Participation means promoting the deceit of triumphant, victorious, sin and disease-free life. This can only be achieved through the retreat behind a religious *persona* or mask, which produces a corporate charade.

At the coal-face of congregational life, the exclusion of suffering results in deception and game-playing. People whose lives may be falling apart are socialized into smiling and 'rejoicing in the Lord'. It is a shallow response, because the pain which they feel unable to exhibit or share is rooted in the depths of their heart, and that level of emotion and honesty is outlawed by convention. When a congregation participates in corporate dishonesty, it is not surprising that they do not experience the passion of God. Christian faith proclaims that God is present in the darkest suffering; perhaps the exclusion of pain is also the exclusion of God.

The revelation received through the crucified Christ teaches that God is present in the midst of human anguish. The only cure for apathy is to allow the silent screams to come to voice, and to face the discomfort which results. Jesus always understood that faithfulness would involve the embrace of the cross. His first followers were not so keen on the idea. When Peter tried to convince him otherwise, Jesus delivered some of his strongest words of rebuke (Matthew 16.23). The path of comfort and apathy is not the path of Christ.

Control

In pre-modern times, hierarchy was accepted as divinely ordained. The basis for the authority of both church and nobility was regarded as being located in the rule of God, and in fact both were respected as instruments of the divine ordering of human life. The Enlightenment, coinciding with the fragmentation of both ecclesiastical and feudal power, relativized all external claims to authority by subjecting them to verification. Democracy was the natural political outworking of Cartesian philosophy. Power and authority did not disappear, however. They shifted from being the heritage of institutions, to becoming the instruments of a new elite.

Knowledge was the new coinage of power, and those who controlled it became the priests and rulers of a secular age. Only certain types of knowledge were admissible: those that were factual, objective and verifiable. Thus the academics and professionals, the discerners of truth, accumulated and regulated power. For the church, of course, there was a huge and painful sense of loss. Used to wielding great authority in the affairs of the world, the ecclesiastical institution did not take kindly to being pushed to the margins.

The church, being a canny player with a long history of survival, adapted itself to the new environment. If power could not be exercised in society at large, it could at least be maintained within the church. But new rules applied. The claim to authority could still be invoked, but it was not so readily accepted by the faithful as in earlier times. Under modernism, the basis of authority was knowledge. Because of this, theology and doctrine assumed new importance. Those who controlled what was right and true would be the arbiters of power. Theological education was of greater significance than apostolic succession, and theological education was in the hands of the clergy.

History has moved on, and modernism itself is in a state of collapse (see Chapter 7). One of postmodernism's sharpest critiques derives from the recognition of the alliance between knowledge and power. The specification of what type of knowledge is admissible in the public realm has been a very effective means of retaining power within a select group. Postmodernists, led by feminists, blacks and liberationists, have taken a close look at who is in the room where the decisions are being made. Their discovery is that the occupants are almost all white, male, wealthy, intellectual heterosexuals. The response has been to subvert the whole process by throwing the doors open, and allowing anyone into the room.

The church, however, is guarding its own doors very closely. Orthodoxy and control are still very much on the agenda. Within the Catholic Church, Cardinal Ratzinger's scrupulosity in his guarding of doctrine typifies the ecclesiastical heavy-handedness. Not only are radicals and subversives excluded from positions of leadership, but even moderates whose only mistake is to raise genuine questions. The underlying assumption seems to be that conservatism is the best course in heavy weather. Presumably, the hope is that the difficulties of the present age may pass, and all will be well again.

This is precisely the approach which will guarantee the demise of the Western church. The people being excluded – the radicals, the artists, the questioners – are exactly the people who are needed for the reformation of the church. These stirrers who trouble the ease of the church can only endure living on the margins for so long. Eventually they drift on, looking for a community where their talents and insights will be appreciated. The very real possibility exists that God may go with them.

Control is simply the operative mechanism of power. It is in the church's understanding and use of power that the real betrayals have occurred. As Walter Wink has painstakingly expounded, the gospel tradition has a unique perspective on power. This perspective seems to have been lost in the transition to Christendom, and never recovered. Jesus introduces the disciples to a kingdom perspective on power in Luke 22.25–7.

But he said to them, 'The kings of the Gentiles lord it over them; and those in authority over them are called benefactors. But not so with you; rather the greatest among you must become like the youngest, and the leader like one who serves.'

This is an inversion of the normal lines of authority and power within human community.

The desire for control and the dispensing of power are very human expressions, and essential to the running of institutions. They are not characteristics of the Christian life. Whenever the church drifts towards institutional form, it is drifting away from the one who was sent for crucifixion by the religious authorities. The pursuit of Christ is a pilgrimage which involves learning how to give up power for the sake of others. It produces a freedom from fear and anxiety, so that followers can relinquish the need for control.

The present reality of the Western church, however, is that power and control are almost defining marks. The dynamics of church life are experienced by many as abusive. It is only in recent years that the mechanics of abuse have been recognized, and with the recognition has come the addition of a new term: spiritual abuse. Alongside the uncovering of the disturbing incidence of sexual abuse perpetrated by clergy, the understanding has dawned that many of the structures and processes of the institutional church are abusive by nature, and encourage the climate in which more explicit expressions of abuse may occur.

It is abusive when people are taught to accept the word of those in authority, and that questioning of that authority is an affront to God. It is abusive when any person or group of persons claims to speak the word of God, and that claim is not subject to discernment by the wider community of believers. It is abusive when decisions are made in secret by a small group of powerholders, and such hierarchical rule is interpreted as being Christian. It can be abusive when difference is demonized, and departure from a prescribed moralistic lifestyle is portrayed as either sin or evil. It can be abusive when control is exercised to ensure the maintenance of the institution.

The Western church has been and is abusive. Many people of integrity and faith have found themselves marginalized and dehumanized by the structures and processes of the church. It is one thing to experience discrimination or contempt from people; it is quite another when it is spiritualized and done in the name of God. The experience leaves church survivors with anger at the way they have been treated, and some struggle to separate their faith from the way it has been turned against them by the religious institution. Such people have been inoculated against the gospel.

Victims of spiritual abuse give voice to the anger and desolation which results:

> I still believe in a caring God, a creator, but I'm not interested in Jesus or church. Church turns God into something abusive.[3]

> The whole way the Church is designed is to mess you up; you have to obey rules and be told how to live your life. You end up repressing your real feelings and opinions simply to be accepted.[4]

The time for defensiveness and justification in the face of such accusations is past. The Western church must be willing to experience the pain of honesty, and confess the dark currents which flow below the surface of church life. Only then will change and growth be possible.

A Community of Grace

As long as the dangerous memory of Jesus is kept alive and accessible within the deadening mills of the Christian factory, there remains the hope that church may become church. However, it may be necessary for much of the formal structure of Western Christianity to 'fall into the ground and die' (John 12.24), in order for new shoots of faith to arise. The challenge to mission in a post-Christian era is how to re-invent a tradition in such a way that it can overcome its apparent staleness, and recapture a sense of freshness. For this to happen, a radical break is necessary; a period of intense reformation which may be experienced by participants as death.

The specific shape of the emerging church is unknown, because the task of reformation has hardly yet begun. Some models of Christian community which contain hope will be described in Chapter 11. In the meantime, however, some general characteristics of the new community may be hinted at. If the church in the West is to survive, it will have to radically reclaim its roots as the community of *Christ*, and subject all of its forms and traditions to the life-giving story of his ministry, death and resurrection.

The community of Christ will be an *alternative* community. It will be a place where cultural values are scrutinized in the light of kingdom values. Athol Gill notes:

> With an emphasis on privatized spirituality and individual decision-making fuelled by the competitive spirit of consumerism, we have come to see the Christian faith as predominantly concerned with the relationship of an individual to God . . . For too long we have been moulded by the dictates and desires of our consumer society. The time has come to say 'no' to these destructive forces so that we might again embrace life with enthusiasm and energy.[5]

A community which reflects the life of Jesus will be a community of *generosity* and *sharing*, of *friendship* and *belonging*, of *mission* and *identity*, of *freedom* and *risk-taking*. As such it cannot but help stand out against the deeply held values of Western culture.

The community of Christ will be a community of *passion*, in both senses of the word. It will be a place where suffering is accepted and given grounding and meaning through the cross. Those who suffer will find in it a place of refuge and acceptance. It will also be a community where life is both affirmed and celebrated; where the words of Jesus are taken seriously: 'I came that they may have life, and have it abundantly' (John 10.10).

The community of Christ will be a community of *partnership*,[6] where the dignity of all and their right to participate is upheld. It will be a non-hierarchical community; a place where service and respect are put ahead of control and status. To use Scott Peck's description, it will be 'a group of all leaders'.[7] The effective power will be love, a disarming vulnerability which lays down its own agenda for the sake of the other.

As it stands, these aspects of following Jesus must stand as agenda rather than as marks of the confessing church. The liberating gospel is smothered within the religious institution. James K. Baxter, poet and founder of an open Christian community in New Zealand, writes:

... I tell my Catholic visitors
The chestnut explains to us our own religion

With the nut of love well hidden under spikes of fear[8]

It is the task of the Western church to prise open the chestnut and grasp the 'nut of love', so that it might be both lived out and shared with the world. This simple but painful task will require courage and determination. The reluctance to begin may be explained with a parable of Kierkegaard's:[9]

A certain flock of geese lived together in a barnyard with great high walls around it. Because the corn was good and the barnyard was secure, these geese would never take a risk. One day a philosopher goose came among them. He was a very good philosopher and every week they listened quietly and attentively to his learned discourses. 'My fellow travellers on the way of life,' he would say, 'can you seriously imagine that this barnyard, with great high walls around it, is all there is to existence?

'I tell you, there is another and a greater world outside, a world of which we are only dimly aware. Our forefathers knew of this outside world. For did they not stretch their wings and fly across the trackless wastes of desert and ocean, of green valley and wooded hill? But alas, here we remain in this barnyard, our wings folded and tucked into our sides, as we are content to puddle in the mud, never lifting our eyes to the heavens which should be our home.

The geese thought this was very fine lecturing. 'How poetical,' they thought. 'How profoundly existential. What a flawless summary of the mystery of existence.' Often the philosopher spoke of the advantages of flight, calling on the geese to be what they were. After all, they had wings, he pointed out. What were wings for, but to fly with? Often he reflected on the beauty and the wonder of life outside the barnyard, and the freedom of the skies.

And every week the geese were uplifted, inspired, moved by the philosopher's message. They hung on his every word. They devoted hours, weeks, months to a thoroughgoing analysis and critical evaluation of his doctrines. They produced learned treatises on the ethical and spiritual implications of flight. All this they did. But one thing they never did. They did not fly! For the corn was good, and the barnyard was secure!

5

Holiness – Above and Apart

–

Peter struggled to accept the Spirit's invitation on the rooftop in Joppa, because of the tradition of holiness which he had inherited. Perhaps the central theme of his Jewish faith was the holiness of God, and the strict protocol required for sinful humans to have any contact with God. Alongside this respect for the divine was the understanding that the children of Israel were a people chosen by God, a holy race (Deuteronomy 7.6). Faithfulness therefore involved maintaining personal and corporate holiness:

> You shall be holy to me; for I the Lord am holy, and I have separated you from the other peoples to be mine. (Leviticus 20.26)

Such holiness was guarded through the establishment of clear boundaries; boundaries which Peter was understandably reluctant to cross.

The crisis of Acts 10 is not only a strategic crisis in terms of mission; it is also a theological crisis of the first order, for it relativizes all prior conceptions of holiness. In fact, the doctrine of holiness had already been torn asunder by the teaching and ministry of Jesus. But the radical implications of his message had not yet been comprehended by the community. It is not easy to reinterpret a tenet of belief which has such claims to centrality as that of holiness.

The Old Testament view of mission was entirely consistent with its understanding of holiness. There, where the conversion of the nations was envisaged, it was a picture of the world streaming toward Jerusalem. There they would be converted, and learn what it meant to be a child of God, and how to live in an acceptable manner:

Many peoples shall come and say,
'Come, let us go up to the mountain of the Lord,
to the house of the God of Jacob;
that he might teach us his ways
and that we may walk in his paths.'

(Isaiah 2.3)

The people of God could still maintain their stance of separation, because those to be converted would come onto their turf.

Perhaps we have underestimated the extent of discontinuity evidenced by the incarnation, attested to in the New Testament.[1] When God moves toward humanity, and takes up residence on 'our turf',[2] then the emphasis shifts from *separation* to *involvement*. I do not think it does violence to the scriptural material to suggest that there is a qualitative change in the concept of holiness from the Old Testament to the New. Jesus introduces a radically new understanding of holiness; the Pharisees and Scribes recoil from it; Peter agonizes over its implications; and the contemporary church has yet to accept it fully. In order to comprehend this disjunction, we must first look at traditional concepts of holiness, drawn largely from the Old Testament, and particularly evidenced by the Priestly Code.[3]

Be Ye Holy

Traditional concepts of holiness were based on the 'otherness' of God. God was seen as great and terrible, so completely different from humanity that to look on the divine visage was to die (Judges 13.22). Encounter with the holy God was a dangerous business, to be compared with high voltage electricity. Insulation was necessary, in the form of various kinds of mediation: priest, ark, sacrifice, etc. Even then, caution would be advised; Uzziah is struck dead when he touches the ark of the covenant in order to

73

steady it (2 Samuel 6.6–11). The 'fear of the Lord' is a genuine experience for the chosen people of Yahweh.

In order to preserve this holiness, certain people, objects and seasons are to be kept *separate* for the Lord.[4] Priests are to be separated from the ordinary people (Numbers 8.14), the firstborn are to be kept apart for God (Exodus 13.12), a menstruating woman is to be isolated for seven days as unclean, as well as everything she touches (Leviticus 15.19–24), and the sabbath and specified festivals are to be reserved for God (Leviticus 23). That only certain foods were to be consumed, we have already established. The underlying principle was clear: 'You shall be holy, for I the Lord your God am holy' (Leviticus 19.2). And whatever was holy needed to be kept apart from all that was not.

'Come apart' is the resounding call to holiness not only in the Old Testament, but also in many Christian devotional books on the subject. It flows fairly easily from this injunction to the idea that isolation is a sign of godliness. There is, obviously, good scriptural support for such a view, and it is one that is attractive to groups which are already marginalized, in that it legitimates their superiority. The dangers of the approach are everywhere in history, from the stories of the genocide in Canaan (Deuteronomy 20.16–18), to the purification of the Third Reich and the experiment of Apartheid in South Africa.

Separation and mission are not easily compatible. It is no coincidence that our Acts 10 passage, which is so central to the missiological era, confronts the traditional understandings of holiness. Separation is a function of preservation, and the impetus to preservation is far from the call to mission. The church has for much of its history accepted uncritically the separatist approach to holiness. In so doing, it has cut itself off from the world which God loves and has given all to reclaim. It is imperative to the renewal of mission that the church reconsider its separatism in the light of Jesus.

The traditional (and, it must be said, in part biblical) attitude to holiness, betrays a deep *dualism*. Dualism is the dichotomizing of existence into opposing categories: good and evil, body and spirit, light and darkness. The central dualism inhabiting Christian concepts of holiness (in common with many other religions) is that of sacred and profane. This in turn is based on the inherited tradition of Judaism. In Pharisaic Judaism, there were many potential sources of contamination for the unsuspecting: lepers, ritually unclean vessels or food, women and sinners. Purity required avoidance, and if breached, atonement through ritual purification.

This distinction between clean and unclean has in Christian thought accumulated an additional dualism: that of body and spirit. This one is not inherited from Judaism at all, but rather from the influence of Hellenism on the early church. Greek thought, following Plato, reified the spiritual as somehow separate from the earthly and bodily, and counted it as inherently superior. The combination of these dualisms has had the effect of producing a tortured Christian response to many normal aspects of human life; in particular, to sexuality. For all the majesty of Augustine, one wishes his sexual anguish had remained his private affair.

The unfortunate legacy is a Christian view of holiness as some sort of ethereal and disembodied existence, in isolation from potential contaminants. It produces disciples who withdraw from the world and contact with sinners, and punish themselves under impossibly ascetic regimes which make little provision for human fallibility. Such an approach to serving God produces a great deal of psychological pressure, with cycles of abstention, transgression and guilt. Those who experience this without any deep encounter with the grace of God may justifiably suspect that Christianity is inherently oppressive.

Illustration of this approach to holiness, popularized in Evangelicalism (particularly in the Keswick Movement), is provided by the following injunction from J. C. Ryle:

A holy man will follow after *temperance and self-denial*. He will labour to mortify the desires of his body – to crucify his flesh with his affectations and lusts – to curb his passions – to restrain his carnal inclinations, lest at any time they break loose.[5]

The view of physical existence portrayed here is of an altruistic spirit inhabiting a treacherous body which is a virtual time-bomb; liable to detonate at any moment if not handled with extreme caution.

This traditional understanding of holiness is further shaped by a concern for *purification*, which borders dangerously on the notion that it is possible for believers to attain sinlessness. Such thinking is usually to be found under the heading of sanctification. It walks a dangerous line, recognizing that claims to absolute sinlessness would be arrogant and potentially blasphemous, while appearing reluctant to let go of the possibility altogether:

> The word 'perfect' can be applied to our intentions and motives. When flesh crucifixion has taken place and is maintained, then all the fallen powers of spirit, soul, and body are made pure and kept pure, even though through ignorance or other infirmity we exercise them in ways which may be mistaken ... The truly sanctified soul, who is continuing in this grace, will not wilfully sin, but is liable to fall through some form of ignorance.[6]

These views are of course somewhat dated. However, they have had a deep and abiding influence on the way in which Christians relate to the world around them. The quest for purification involves separation from potential sources of temptation, and the world is seen as the source of them:

> He must fight *the world*. The subtle influence of that mighty enemy must be daily resisted, and without a daily battle can never be overcome. The love of the world's good things ... all these are spiritual forces which beset

the Christian continually on his way to heaven, and must be conquered.[7]

When the world is regarded as enemy,[8] it is not surprising that mission falters. When followers of Christ regard daily life as a minefield which threatens their purity, it is only to be suspected that they will be fearful and recalcitrant in their dealings with 'outsiders'.

A Man for Others

Far from keeping the requisite distance from potential sources of contamination, Jesus was known as 'a glutton and a drunkard, *a friend of tax collectors and sinners*' (Matthew 11.19). Such friendship with the ritually unclean was a great stumbling-block to the religious leaders of the day. As Athol Gill notes, the departure from traditional concepts of holiness was striking:

> The distinctive feature of the ministry of Jesus was that while it was open to everyone it was directed primarily towards those whom the orthodox, the religious establishment, considered to be beyond the fringes of respectability.[9]

Jesus' own reputation suffered because of the sort of people he associated with. The company he kept cast serious doubts on his character:

> Jesus accepted public sinners – plainly spoken, criminals – and was seen 'in bad company'. He ate and drank with disreputable people. So he was regarded as dishonourable and lawless.[10]

It is simply not possible to reconcile Jesus' ministry with traditional concepts of holiness. But if we see Jesus as the image of God (Colossians 1.15), and Scripture assures us that God is holy, then we must surely address our concepts of what it means to be holy. This is the essential Christian task – to reinterpret inherited concepts of God in the light of Christ.

If we are to take this task seriously, then there is no way that a view of holiness as separation can be maintained. Jesus seems to have an almost callous disregard for categories of clean and unclean. In his physical contact with lepers, his touch by a menstruating woman, his dialogue with men and women of dubious character, Jesus becomes himself ritually unclean by any normal rendering of Jewish religious practice. Far from keeping himself pure, he seems to delight in placing himself in ambiguous situations, and flouting the dualistic view of the world.

In order to understand Jesus' attitude to holiness, we need to look at some of his own explanatory comments. The sharpest of these is the direct confrontation with traditional concepts, recorded in Luke 11.37–41:

> While he was speaking, a Pharisee invited him to dine with him; so he went in and took his place at the table. The Pharisee was amazed to see that he did not first wash before dinner. Then the Lord said to him, 'Now you Pharisees clean the outside of the cup and of the dish, but inside you are full of greed and wickedness. You fools! Did not the one who made the outside make the inside also? So give for alms those things that are within; and see, everything will be clean for you.'

The effect of this teaching is to relocate the evaluation of holiness from external behaviour to an internal orientation of the heart. Particularly significant is Jesus' assurance that if the inside is clean, then 'everything will be clean for you'.

A second incident, again involving a confrontation with Pharisaic Judaism, is even more enlightening:

> And as he sat at dinner in the house, many tax collectors

and sinners came and were sitting with him and his disciples. When the Pharisees saw this, they said to his disciples, 'Why does your teacher eat with tax collectors and sinners?' But when he heard this, he said, 'Those who are well have no need of a physician, but those who are sick. Go and learn what this means, "I desire mercy, and not sacrifice." For I have come to call not the righteous but sinners.' (Matthew 9.10–13)

Here is the interpretive key for understanding Jesus' mixing with sinners and outcasts; he does so because he has come for their sake. Christ's mission, the mission of God, sees the offering of love and forgiveness to sinners as paramount. If God is wholly other, then that otherness is to be made known in the context of sinful humanity, rather than separated from it.

Another feature of Jesus' demonstration of holiness, this time consistent with Jewish thinking, is his *earthed spirituality*. His approach to life and faith is neither ascetic nor incorporeal. If Jesus is a holy man, his holiness is grounded and accessible. His first miracle, according to John, is to produce more wine for a wedding (John 2.1–11). There he is enjoying himself in the midst of a very human social celebration. His provision of wine is no niggardly thing, either; the party is well gone, and there is at least the hint that some of the celebrants are well gone themselves (v. 10) when Jesus produces another 600 litres of good wine.

His reputation as a glutton and a drunkard may well have something to do with his fondness for sitting around the table with his friends, eating and drinking. In the gospels alone, the words 'eat' or 'eating' are found 107 times, and 'drink' or 'drinking' some 55 times. A great deal of Jesus' teaching takes place around the table, while he is enjoying the company of friends. As a precursor of both the eucharist and the messianic feast, this substantive celebration of the goodness of life is no peripheral activity in the ministry of Jesus:

Mission does not mean only proclamation, teaching, and healing, but it also involves eating and drinking. Mission happens through community in eating and drinking. Hope is eaten and drunk. This is the eating and drinking mission of the kingdom.[11]

We have already commented on the sort of people Jesus surrounded himself with, and whose company he seems to have enjoyed. Though unmarried, Jesus related freely and easily with women, who seem to have been a part of his following throughout his ministry. When his friend Mary massages Jesus' feet with expensive balm, and then wipes them with her hair, Jesus shows none of the sexual tension or physical embarrassment which marks many of his later followers. Even when risen from the dead, Jesus is no spectre, but eats fish with his friends so that they might recognize him (John 21.1–14).

It would seem, then, that Jesus does not share the nervousness toward temptation and the world which is such a central strand of traditional attitudes to holiness. And yet, undeniably, he is the pattern for Christian life and holiness. That being so, his holiness must spring from a different source than that evidenced by the Priestly Code in the Old Testament. The clue to this holiness has been presaged above; Jesus' holiness is not a function of his behaviour at all, but of some *inner quality* in his life. It has its source in his relationship with the heart of the Trinity.

Even though Jesus freely mixed with 'sinners', there was a quality about his life and teaching which marked him out. We read that people were astonished because Jesus taught them as one having authority (Matthew 7.29; Mark 1.22). Clearly this sense of authority was not based on any external symbols of status or power. Rather it was, for want of a better term, located in the force of his character. The reason he created such a fuss was that even those who opposed him were aware of the power of life and goodness which he exhibited.

This provides a new twist on holiness as separation, one which may be dimly present in the previous tradition. It is separation *to*, rather than separation *from*. Jesus is holy not because he isolates himself from either people or the world, nor because of some elaborate system of ritual purification. He is holy because he is consumed with passion for both God and the world. Mission is a fire in his heart and a hammer in his bones:

> But he said to them, 'I have food to eat that you do not know about.' So the disciples said to one another, 'surely no one has brought him something to eat?' Jesus said to them, 'My food is to do the will of him who sent me to complete his work.' (John 4.32–4)

Because the love of God is burning in his heart, Jesus is holy. And because he is holy, all the world has become clean to him.

This type of holiness is eminently suited to, and to a certain extent derives from, mission. It is a holiness which is portable, accessible and inviolable. It need not fear contamination because it proceeds outward from the heart. Its source and spring is hidden from the world, but its benefit still touches the world.

Making God Present

Peter's reluctance to partake of proscribed foods was consistent with his received tradition of holiness. It grew from his separatist approach to piety, which divided the world into clean and unclean. His attitude to gentiles derived from the same source: a division between insiders and outsiders. Even though Peter had followed Jesus through Palestine, and seen and heard the confrontation with orthodoxy which ensued, the implications of Jesus' mission and teaching did not hit home until his meeting with Cornelius.

Somewhere between then and now, the Western church

has lost its way and reverted to a dualistic perspective on the world. It is time the church rediscovered what it means to be the 'friend of tax collectors and sinners'. Only when the Christian view of holiness is informed by the teaching of Jesus will the church be equipped to encounter the world in missionary orientation. This will not happen without the same sort of psychological and theological tension which anguished Peter. But as has been argued, the alternative to painful change may well be a comfortable death.

A Christian understanding of holiness will mean *freedom from fear*. Evangelical churchgoers in particular seem to live fearful and anxious lives. As Pete Ward notes, 'Many evangelical Christians experience aspects of contemporary society as extremely threatening.'[12] The underlying view of holiness which drives such fear is that one is constantly at risk of contamination from outside sources. Television, films, politics, 'dirty talk' from workmates; all are potential avenues of corruption, and therefore to be avoided. The world outside the church is seen as an intimidating and malevolent arena.

The good news in Jesus Christ is that fearfulness has come to an end. The good world, created by God, distorted by sin and evil, has been redeemed in Christ. Security arises through relationship with Christ, and this is not at threat from external sources. As our Lord before us, we are able to enter into all sorts of situations of sin and ambiguity without fear of contamination. The life of Christ is a life free from anxiety:

> Love has been perfected among us in this: that we may have boldness on the day of judgement, because as he is, so are we in this world. There is no fear in love, but perfect love casts out fear. (1 John 4.17, 18)

The secret of this freedom from fear lies in a strong sense of our *identity in Christ*. Jesus' holiness, as we have established, was based on an inner quality; his sense of relationship within the Trinity, and a burning impetus to mission. Our own holiness will consist in nothing more nor less than God made present through our relationship to Christ, and our consequent commitment to God's mission. In Colossians, Paul unfolds the central mystery of the faith, unknown among previous generations, but now made known even among the gentiles. It is simple: 'Christ in you, the hope of glory' (Colossians 1.27).

Any holiness we may lay claim to comes not from our own behaviour or moral virtue. It consists entirely in our participation in Christ, and our consequent sharing in his holy life (1 Corinthians 1.30). God was incarnate in Christ, and Christ is being made incarnate in his followers: 'formed in you' (Galatians 4.16). If indeed we are in Christ, and participants in his life, then we are already holy by virtue of that fact. Our responsibility consists in maintaining our relationship with Christ, not in preserving ourselves from sin. It is only when we trust in Christ within us rather than our own resources that the concept of holiness has any hope for us.

Here is the central truth of Christian holiness: it consists not in *behaviour*, but in *identity*. Identity will of course influence behaviour. But whereas behaviour is external and open to influence from a variety of factors, identity is rooted in the core of a person, and to a large extent inviolable. When we know that we are safe in Christ, we are free to go wherever we want and mix with whoever we find, and do it without fear. Our orientation will be one of mission: concerned not with isolating and protecting our inner purity, but with finding ways to make the Christ who is within us accessible to others.

At a recent conference on mission, a speaker made use of the lyrics of a song by singer/songwriter Lorina Harding – 'The Not-So-Righteous Café'. The controversy which was provoked is indicative of the nervousness felt about a mission approach which reflects Jesus' own ministry. With the generous permission of Lorina, I reprint some of the lyrics here. They encapsulate much of the argument being proffered in this chapter.

THE NOT-SO-RIGHTEOUS CAFÉ

Now there was this dinner at this ritzy café
And all of the righteous had been invited there that day,
And they were feeling so smug about their right to heaven
That they didn't notice someone at table number seven.

They weren't too sure why they'd been invited there,
But hey the food was free and there was drink to spare;
And they'd just said grace and were about to imbibe
When a few more guests began to arrive.

In came a man who was obviously drunk
And it was plain to everyone the depths to which he'd sunk,
And it was hard to imagine he'd ever been human once.
And the righteous rose up and spoke in one voice,
And said:

Hey drunkard, you can't come in here –
Your clothes are a mess and you stink of beer;
And you're gonna cause trouble, that's absolutely clear.
But a voice from seven said, 'Come sit with me.'

Chorus:
Open your heart and open your eyes,
This banquet is free, and not just some prize;
The first shall be last, hey, what a surprise –
At the not-so-righteous café.

Then in walked Tracy in a tight red dress;
She had legs that reached right up to her neck,
And from the look on some faces they'd already met.
And the righteous rose up and they spoke in one voice,
Saying:

Hey hooker, you can't come in here –

84

You'll probably bite if we get too near;
And God is gonna get you for choosing that career.
But a voice from seven said, 'Come over here.'

Chorus

If holiness is to be based on identity in Christ, it means that our *piety is portable*. Holiness, which is nothing other than the presence of God, is not tied to places, events, seasons or even moralities. Rather it is tied to people, who carry Christ within them. These people are separated *to God*, not *from the world*. They live in a very messy world, not in fear, but in love. Wherever they go, Christ is with them, because Christ is within them. And because Christ is within them, they are able to recognize his work and presence amongst 'gentiles' and other outsiders.

It should already be apparent that understanding holiness in this way is much more conducive to mission than is an attitude which leads Christians to regard people with suspicion and mistrust. There can be no mission where there is no contact, and many Christians in the West today are imprisoned and isolated by an unnecessary concern for their own sanctification. These bearers of the precious 'treasure' of Christ's presence have become locked into a theological outlook which prevents them from sharing it with the people who are most hungry and 'sick'.

The holiness of Jesus, and its missionary consequence, will of course take us *beyond safety*. It leads us, like Peter, into situations where all the certainties are gone. We must enter environments which are morally and theologically ambiguous, and in which we find ourselves distinctly uncomfortable. God is no respecter of boundaries, and the unfolding history of mission is one of ever-expanding ripples in which the love of God encounters increasingly more unlikely people and situations. There are legitimate concerns for safety, but there is also the legitimate call of Jesus to give up our safety for the sake of others.

Christians sometimes give the impression that they are

more protective of the reputation of God than God is. As the Bible affirms, God is love, and the expression of love is the highest priority in the divine mission. Many people of faith, ostensibly evangelistic at heart, have forgotten the fundamental premise of John 3.16: 'For God so loved the world'. The love of God resulted in Jesus rubbing shoulders with prostitutes and lepers. The same love in us may lead us beyond our comfort zones.

> Just being where other people are can be painful: it might take us into places we would not normally venture ... Jesus calls us to evangelize in the world, sharing the good news on other people's terms, in territory where we are vulnerable, and willingly so.[13]

Many years ago, I worked as a Trainee Linesman for the telephone company. I had recently become a Christian, and was very keen in my faith. I was deeply immersed in evangelical orthodoxy, from quiet-time to memory verses. At my place of work, I was scrupulous in my behaviour, seeking at all times to give a good witness by such measures as refraining from swearing and making my displeasure known when others around me swore. I felt myself to be an alien in a foreign land. I did my best to share my faith with my workmates, so much so that it was often difficult to find anyone who would share a van with me.

I certainly provided a witness. I witnessed to my self-righteousness, my attitude of superiority, my moralistic lack of friendship with my colleagues, and to the irrelevance of Christianity to ordinary people who knew themselves to be far from perfect. I often look back at that period of my life and cringe. At the same yard was another Christian man; a Maori Pentecostal. He was friendly, affable, accepting of others, and always joined in on fun or social occasions. He sometimes had a drink or a smoke in order to express his participation. This man was both popular and respected.

At the time, I was suspicious of my Christian brother's commitment to Christ. It took some years before I realized that he was a long way ahead of me in his pursuit of Jesus. One of the things he used to do was to learn simple greetings in a huge range of different languages. I remember him explaining that it was always good to let people know that you were prepared to go a little way toward meeting them on their ground. He was, of course, passionate about Jesus, and found many opportunities to talk about him to the people he worked with. This man was holy in the true sense of the word, though he would not have claimed it for himself. He was, he would tell you, a sinner at heart.

If holiness is an essential quality of who God is, and Jesus is the revelation of God in humanity, then we see in Jesus the epitome of holiness. To the extent that we share in the life of Christ, we will be participants in that holiness. It is not a quality we can organize for ourselves; it is more like a byproduct of devotion to Christ. And devotion to Christ is expressed not in statements of belief, but in leaving behind our securities and following him into the world, sharing his compassion for those who are loved by God and do not yet know it. True holiness will not keep us from the world, but drive us into it in faith.

6

Dreaming the Forbidden Dream

—

The last few chapters have directed an extended critique at the form and practice of the Western church. Some indications have also been provided of the changes necessary to address the shortcomings of the institutional church. Recovering from the abuses of the past, however, is not in itself enough. The church must move into an entirely new era, and somehow retain a missiological orientation. The chapter following this one will look in some detail at the emerging culture. For the meantime, it is necessary to provide a methodological foundation for the thoroughgoing reformation which is required.

Vision is a romantic and oft-abused term. Its discontinuity with the present is useful to a wide range of people who wish to pursue their own ends, and have others follow them. Simply because such charismatic leaders speak in terms of 'vision', does not make their proposals genuinely so. Discerning the validity of vision is no easy task, except in retrospect. The true visionary shares many attributes with those who are psychiatrically ill, and may only be validated by history. Even so, there are some elements of authentic vision which can be identified, and to that task we now turn.

The Mechanics of Vision

It may well be the sign of a hopelessly modernist and analytical mind to speak of the 'mechanics' of vision. Even so, it is helpful to examine in greater detail the way in which vision operates in leading a faith community forward. In considering the following aspects of vision, I am indebted beyond measure to Walter Brueggemann and his brilliant insights contained in the slim volume *The Prophetic Imagi-*

nation. His Old Testament scholarship and synthetic theologizing have produced a book which is in itself visionary.

THE PRECURSOR OF VISION: NUMBNESS

Vision does not fare well in a situation of universal contentment. The underlying precondition of vision is a dysfunctional context. It does not follow, however, that participants in a dysfunctional community will recognize that there are problems. On the contrary, when the distorted situation has continued for some time, those involved may have a heavy psychological investment in keeping reality just the way it is. The prospect of change becomes threatening in direct proportion to the amount of change which is necessary.

It is not necessarily the case that oppressed people are longing for liberation. As Freire has noted, people who are bowed-down may often provide virulent opposition to any would-be liberator.[1] The prevailing attitude is more likely to be one of apathy and numbness, in which even the prospect of change is denied. It becomes safer to continue to exist in a situation which may be awful, but in which at least the rules are familiar, than to entertain the possibility of transformation which is unknown and therefore dangerous.

THE POWER OF VISION: IMAGINATION

The mythic power of the *status quo*, upheld by those who have an investment in its continuation, is termed 'royal consciousness' by Brueggemann. It has the power to sap energy and prevent change, by stifling imagination:

> We need to ask if our consciousness and imagination have been so assaulted and coopted by the royal consciousness that we have been robbed of the courage or power to think an alternative thought.[2]

The power of vision therefore lies in the ability to *imagine* an alternative to the existing reality; in the terms of this book, to think outside the square. The point of entry of change into a social condition of numbness is that of imagination.

Similarly, if vision has any power to change reality, it is in the arena of imagination. The language of vision is symbol, myth and poetry. In the use of these tools, the possibility arises that people may once again entertain the dream that things might be different than they are. Vision, or prophecy as Brueggemann prefers, is nothing other than the operation of an alternative consciousness which allows imagination to introduce the scenario of a future which is different from the present.

THE PAIN OF VISION: GRIEF

When imagination is employed to contemplate an alternative to the *status quo*, it has the effect of shedding light on the deficiencies of the present. To contemplate God's future is to set the immediate foreground against it. For the one (or the community) who is enabled to see, the result is deep pain. To behold the vision, to see as God sees, is to participate in the grieving of God over a lost people.

Jerusalem, Jerusalem,
the city that kills the prophets
and stones those who are sent to it!
How often have I desired to gather your children together
as a hen gathers her brood under her wings,
and you were not willing!

(Matthew 23.37)

Only insiders can engage in prophetic vision of the type we are talking about. The pain they feel is the pain of the insider, lamenting over a situation for which they share responsibility. The task of the prophet, according to Brueggemann, is to give voice to their own grief and that of their people, thereby cutting through the silent numbness.

This denying and deceiving kind of numbness is broken

only by the embrace of negativity, by the public articulation that we are fearful and ashamed of the future we have chosen.[3]

It is the language of grief which is alone capable of producing change; this for two reasons. Firstly, grieving and lament give voice to a pain which is crippling while it remains hidden and silent. And secondly, grief invites participation, where confrontation and anger may produce only resentment and intractability. Such grief, however, is never merely instrumental – it arises from the abiding pain experienced by those who have seen the poverty of 'normal' life against the horizon of God's future.

THE PROCESS OF VISION: ANTICIPATION

Being stuck in grief is a problem both personally and corporately. The articulation of vision necessarily moves people to despair, but that is not the end toward which it moves. The intended outcome is that of change – a movement in the direction of the alternative future which has been envisaged. Before communities can move forward, however, they must see that there is some path for them to tread. An unexperienced future is always threatening (Numbers 14.1–4), whereas that which is seen in part is reassuring and even inviting.

Implementing vision therefore requires the anticipation of the future in tangible forms. Models of the vision give some concrete form to what is being described, and also provide a contrast with the present. When John the Baptist sends messengers to ask Jesus if he is the Christ, Jesus replies:

Go and tell John what you have seen and heard: the blind receive their sight, the lame walk, the lepers are cleansed, the deaf hear, the dead are raised, the poor have good news brought to them. (Luke 7.22)

These are visible signs of the kingdom which Jesus proclaimed; he gave flesh to the vision by anticipating it in his own ministry. Those who have seen an alternative way of living need to give shape to it by participating in building what Athol Gill has termed 'parables of the future'.[4] In terms of the methodology of vision, this may well be the most significant part.

THE PRICE OF VISION: MISUNDERSTANDING

There is, naturally, resistance to change from those who have a stake in preserving things the way they are. These architects of the 'royal consciousness' will use every means at their disposal to preserve their base of status and power. The cost of promoting vision is misunderstanding at the very least; often it involves confrontation and rejection. Our own biblical history of the prophets shows that they are almost universally rejected. Jesus' own experience is an example of such rejection: 'He came to what was his own, and his own people did not accept him' (John 1.11).

Misunderstanding is the necessary corollary of those who operate from vision. It would be naive to get involved in the process without recognizing the cost. Announcing the future is the same as denouncing the present, depending on which perspective you are looking from. Vision and those associated with it are subversives, and will be regarded as such by the establishment. Perhaps even more painful is the likelihood that they will be misunderstood and rejected by members of their own community, people whom they love and respect. It is not surprising, in this light, that genuine visionaries are thin on the ground.

THE PRODUCT OF VISION: HOPE

The numbness of living death is a condition of despair, and the absence of hope. Hope requires that the future be open, but the power-holders cannot allow this:

As a beginning point it may be affirmed that the royal consciousness militates against hope ... The present ordering, and by derivation the present regime, claims to be the full and final ordering. That claim means there can be no future that either calls the present into question or promises a way out of it.[5]

When alternative visions of existence arise, they transform the future from oppressive *fate* to liberating *destiny*.[6] Hope is introduced to the situation of ordinary people, because the possibility of change has been presented.

Vision leads to an expanding capacity for hope, whereas the lack of it increases despair. It is the introduction of hope into a previously closed situation which is the true mark of vision. People who have been bowed down and passive begin to take responsibility and act within their own world. Only in this condition can people realize the potential of their humanity: to be free agents invited to work with God in welcoming the coming age, the kingdom of God. That vision is the foundation of all others.

These, then, are some of the identifiable aspects of the dynamic process of introducing prophetic vision to a closed situation. The argument of this book is that the church stands historically in one of those closed epochs which calls for vision and reformation.

Finding a Way Forward

While the thesis of the book is that the Western church is dying, it would not be worth writing if there were no hope for change. The current situation is indeed dire, and continuation along existing paths may well result in practical non-existence. But the recognition of impending calamity may just function as a wake-up call for us. If so, then a comprehensive reform of the Western church is called for. That is the scope of the remainder of this book.

It is vital that would-be reformers are in touch with the *Zeitgeist*, the spirit of the age. They must be participants in their cultural history; people who feel the dangers and achievements of a particular period of history as their own. It is impossible to articulate the captivity or deathliness of any situation when standing on the outside of it. Whether it be the despairing resignation of exiles in Babylon, or the stifling weight of institutional religion in pre-modern Germany, those who seek to bring change must understand deeply that which they hope to transform.

Neither is it enough in our pluralist situation to understand only the life of the faith community. One must be in touch with the broader movements of our entire Western culture; have some understanding of phenomena as diverse as body-art and retail therapy. Too often in recent times Christians have stood over against the rest of society and criticized from a distance. This mud-slinging is performed in both ignorance and isolation. It has the effect of driving the recipients of the criticism further into resentment and despair.

On the other hand, participants in the culture such as Douglas Coupland are able to identify aspects of our common existence in a way that invokes recognition and lament. Take, for example, his catalogue of 'new temptations':

instant wealth
emotionally disengaged sex
information overload
belief in the ability of ingested substances to alter the aura of one's flesh or personality architecture
neglect of the maintenance of democracy
wilful ignorance of history
body manipulation
wilful rejection of reflection
body envy

belief that spectacle is reality
vicarious living through celebrities
rejection of sentiment
unwillingness to assign hierarchy to values[7]

This is a genuine 'discerning of the times' which gives voice
to the numbness and hopelessness of the culture. Insight of
this order is not necessarily the result of sharp analytical
tools; its main pre-requisite is involvement and empathy.

DREAMING THE FORBIDDEN DREAM

Carl Gustav Jung, in his *Memories, Dreams and Reflections*,
tells the story of a waking dream which he had while still a
schoolboy.[8] It was a perfect day; blue skies, abundant
sunshine and birds singing. He was in Cathedral Square,
and could see the roof of the cathedral shining in the sun.
And there in heaven, above the church, God sits on a golden
throne. As Jung watches, an event takes place which he
refuses to admit into his consciousness: 'Here came a great
hole in my thoughts, and a choking sensation.'

For several days, he carries the terror of his final vision
with him. Many times he begins to recall the episode, and
has to fight to keep it from reaching its conclusion. The
psychic strain on Jung is enormous. He knows that if he
allows the forbidden dream to enter his mind, it will change
his life for ever. Finally, he can no longer withstand it, and
the censured finale streams into his field of vision. The
cathedral is there, the sky is blue, the birds are singing,
God is in heaven. Then, to Jung's horror, God defecates; a
great turd falls out of heaven onto the church, shattering its
roof and bursting its walls.

It was at this point in his development that Jung, son of a
pastor, realized that God existed in separation from the
church. It allowed the young psychoanalyst to contemplate
the reality of the divine despite his disdain for the conservative German church which he had experienced:

the immediate living God who stands, omnipotent and free, above His Bible and His Church, who calls upon man to partake of His freedom, and can force him to renounce his own views and convictions in order to fulfill without reserve the command of God. In His trial of human courage God refuses to abide by traditions, no matter how sacred.[9]

While Jung's dream may be more offensive to Christians than Peter's vision, the two are of a similar order. They introduce the unthinkable and verge on the blasphemous. Nevertheless, they also celebrate the freedom of God to be God, and to operate at times in distinction from the propriety of the faith community.

In times of desperation or stagnation, it may be that we are called upon to dream forbidden dreams. Certainly the kingdom of God, as represented by Jesus' Sermon on the Mount, remains counter-cultural both inside and outside the church. But what specific forms might this dream have for our place and time? Perhaps we too must admit the unimaginable into our consciousness, if we are to permit God to lead us forward. This exercise is one of imagination and creativity. It is possible that the required vision will arise in unlikely places; amongst artists and fringe-dwellers, rather than theologians and strategists.

SPEAKING THE TRUTH

The leading edge of change comes from those who are prepared to speak the truth, however unpopular that may be. Those who dream dreams and see visions will inevitably have some cutting insights into the present. When they describe what they are seeing, they will engender resistance from the power-holders and symbol-makers of the existing order. Let no one underestimate the power of social sanction which still exists to silence those who challenge the powerful. Great courage is required to speak the truth in the face of a collective lie, and there are no guarantees that truth will prevail.

What is certain is that no change can take place without the puncturing of deceptive mythology. The fable of The Emperor's Clothes is more than a children's story. The community of Christ might become a place of truth-telling within the wider society, but it might also share the fate of its founder if it were to do so. Instead, the Western church has invested heavily in the prevalent myths of consumerism and individualism, and now acts in concert with the predominant lie-tellers. Consequently the church itself is in need of honest voices, but it is unlikely to welcome them in the short term.

Dennis Arcand, in his magnificent film *Jesus of Montreal*, has the Jesus figure boiling over with anger during auditioning for a television beer commercial, in which a struggling actress is taunted to 'show us your tits'. In rage, he breaks up the television equipment, and chases the producers out of the theatre, flailing them with severed cables. He is a truth-teller. The same character is no less repugnant to the church, where he is betrayed by a sexually active priest who enjoys his exercise of status and power. In artistic expressions such as these, we find an honesty which is sorely needed.

REOWNING THE PAST

One of the advantages of being Christian is that our past is our future. The Jesus who preceded us is the same one who is calling us into the future.[10] Our Christian conviction is that Christ is alpha and omega; that in him we see both beginning and end. The seeds of the future are contained within the life, death and resurrection of Jesus of Nazareth. In finding a way forward, then, our forbidden dreams of the future will need not only to critique the present, but also to find some point of continuity with the past. They will need to be reframed in relation to the Jesus story which is the Christian point of departure.[11]

The strategy called for, modelled inspirationally by Deutero-Isaiah, is one of *radicality*. That is, the reclaiming and reinterpreting of tradition in such a way that it is consistent with its roots and yet adequate to the new situation. Paul of Tarsus was another exponent of the craft. He translated a Jewish messianic tradition into words and pictures which communicated in an entirely different culture, yet without doing violence to the meaning stored in the traditional symbols. Too often we have carried forward the results of Pauline radical theology, rather than the process which he engaged in.

ESTABLISHING TRANSITIONAL STRUCTURES

Anticipating the future requires supportive and transitional structures for the nascent vision. It is generally not the case that one form of response to life and faith dies, and then a new one develops abruptly. For a period the old and the new will exist side by side, a threat to each other and the cause of tension and power-plays. The visionary community needs protective structures, within which it can develop its own self-understanding, free of domination and control from the failing institution. Such tangible structures will also provide a sign of hope to people trapped in old orthodoxies but nervous about stepping out into the unknown.

An illustration from motorway construction may help.[12] When planning a new section of motorway which may cross other streams of traffic, the engineers have a number of factors to consider. One is that they need to maintain existing traffic flows with a minimum of disruption. Another is the preparatory work which is needed for the new roading. The solution is often to keep existing roads in place, while proceeding with the construction of the new in close proximity. Traffic is not diverted onto the new carriageway until all is in place.

In a similar way, existing institutions need to carry the traffic of previous generations, even while new routes are being constructed all around them. In time they will be phased out and become redundant. When it happens, the fresh pathways will be established enough to be able to bear the load put upon them by an increase in travellers. Construction of transitional structures is not as exciting as the planning of new avenues, but it is essential work if reformation is to succeed. Visionaries may be reluctant to be involved in the sheer graft. Without it their visions may well remain private.

THINKING OUTSIDE THE BOX

New situations draw on new resources. Those challenged with the unfamiliar can either yield to despair and passivity (Lamentations), or find themselves stimulated to look for new patterns and solutions (Deutero-Isaiah). While thought and conversation remain locked within the square of convention, existence tends to be predictable and fatalistic. Apprehending vision and implementing it requires a letting go of previous syntheses, and an openness to perceiving reality from different perspectives.

To adopt or encourage this approach is undoubtedly subversive. In Jesus' time, the local establishment was quick to recognize the very real threat to their established power base, and responded accordingly. This fate is not peculiar to Palestinian visionaries; it is not only Jerusalem that 'kills the prophets and stones those who are sent to it' (Matthew 23.37). Those who we view in retrospect as the creative thinkers of the age often die in poverty, captivity or derision. The task of pioneering is by nature a lonely one, but it is one which is desperately needed by the Christian community at the turn of the millennium.

Grazing the Future

God comes out of the future onto our horizon as a sandstorm comes out of the desert. The faith community has always been moving forward, whether geographically or theologically. It only betrays its purpose when it attempts to settle down in history or culture, and begins to make absolutes out of those things which can only ever be transitory. God calls to us from the future, urging us out of our lethargy and self-containment. As Moltmann has poetically stated:

> Those who hope in Christ can no longer put up with reality as it is, but begin to suffer under it, to contradict it. Peace with God means conflict with the world, for the goad of the promised future stabs inexorably into the flesh of every unfulfilled present.[13]

It is one of those seasons of the church when we must risk all to gain all. We can 'no longer put up with reality as it is'. God is calling the Western church beyond its previous boundaries, into entirely new territory. There is no compulsion in a call. We are free to accept or reject it. But if we want to be where God is, then we will have to move beyond the frontiers of the present, and begin to graze the foothills of the future. From this point on in the book, we begin to investigate what that future looks like, and what implications there might be for following Christ in that environment.

7

The Emerging World

—

There is a developing consensus that the West is in the midst of a major cultural transition. In a book playfully titled *Reality Isn't What It Used To Be*, Walter Anderson declares: 'In recent decades we have passed, like Alice slipping through the looking glass, into a new world.'[1] That new world is not universally welcomed. To many reluctant observers, it seems a bizarre and frightening place.

No major cultural transition is sharp or sudden. It takes several generations for one cultural matrix to wane and another to gain sufficient strength to be recognized as an enduring alternative. Nevertheless, it seems to many social analysts that we may be reaching the critical half-way point, where the balance between the dying and the emergent swings in favour of the new cultural matrix. The shift has a certain inexorable quality to it. The tide will come in, and many of the sandcastles of certainty upon which we have built our certainty and identity will no longer be standing when it recedes.

Postmodernity

'Postmodernism' is a slippery word. As one commentator has advised, 'This word has no meaning. Use it as often as possible.'[2] Or again: 'Postmodernism is a contemporary movement. It is strong and fashionable. Over and above this, it is not altogether clear what the devil it is.'[3]

The fact is that the word 'postmodernism' has very little content of its own. It is a sign; a pointer in reference to other concepts, like the word 'north'. It says simply that the previous cultural and philosophic synthesis, 'modernism', is at an end, and something else is emerging to take its place.

101

Because no one knows yet precisely the shape of the future, it is convenient to speak of postmodernism: the force which will follow modernism. The words 'postmodernism' and 'emerging culture' are substantially interchangeable.

Postmodernism, however, has also attached to a philosophical revolution in the realm of epistemology, the science of knowing. Here the names of Derrida, Lyotard, Baudrillard and Rorty are associated with such terms as deconstruction and metanarrative.[4] Although theologians and cultural theorists need to be familiar with such 'philosophic postmodernism', it is not the intention here to examine it in any great depth. We are concerned largely with the cultural face of postmodernism, which although shaped by its philosophic counterpart at many points, remains an independent and more powerful force at the popular level.

It is perhaps necessary to say that many Christian commentators of recent times have exhibited confusion between these two representations of postmodernism. The tendency is to tilt at the windmill of deconstructionism, establish its inherent tendency to a debilitating relativism, and on that basis to dismiss postmodernism altogether as a worthy dialogue partner for Christianity. This is to underestimate the cultural force of postmodernism in the West. We are not speaking of some esoteric epistemological debate which is awaiting Christian approval to proceed, but of the shape of the emerging context in which Christian mission must take place.

We can neither ignore nor dismiss that context. It is rapidly becoming the locus of our faith. The question, therefore, which will focus our attention, is that of understanding the broad parameters of the nascent cultural milieu. The times, as Dylan said, they are a-changin'. We stand on the threshold of the future, looking across the border. Spies have been sent out, and have come back with mixed reports. Perhaps this is a territory of danger and tyranny; perhaps it is the promised land. Only those with the courage to enter it will know.

The Time of our Lives

Describing the future is risky; it is a lot safer to describe the past. In keeping with the spirit of postmodernity, the following outline of the features of the emerging culture is subjective, patchy, non-linear and impressionistic. No claims are made for exhaustiveness or accuracy of description; other writers have attempted this with varying degrees of success, and the results of their work are readily available.[5] The abiding purpose is to begin to make some sense out of the world in which we find ourselves, with the hope that we might find ways to speak about Christ within it.

URBANIZATION

We are at the point in world history where, for the first time, there are more people living in cities than outside of them. Just one hundred and fifty years ago, approximately 2 per cent of the world's population lived in cities.[6] What we have been witnessing in recent times is one of the biggest migrations in human history, with profound effects on the way that people live, act and think. Although urban centres have always functioned as bases of power, it remains true that throughout history most people have formed their values and lifestyles in rural contexts. Now that balance has shifted irreversibly toward the urban.

The significance of this migration is not simply that people are living *in* cities; it is also that they are adopting the culture *of* cities. They are being formed within the culture of *urbanism*, a broad range of responses to the urban environment. Nor is this culture restricted to city-dwellers. The power and reach of the media in forming culture is obvious.[7] What is less obvious is that the values of the media are inevitably urban values. Thus, even those who continue to live in rural areas are being shaped by urbanism.

The cultural values of urbanism are diverse. *Mobility* refers both to the frenetic geographical movement of urbanites, and to the (often false) perception of social mobility. Our jammed transport networks are a symbol of the one; BMWs perhaps a sign of the other. *Anonymity* is a recognition that the huge populations of cities change the way in which we relate to people. Friendships and familial relationships need to be guarded and distinguished from more functional relationships, such as those with workmates or the service station attendant. We tend to choose our social networks, rather than inherit them.

The constant bombardment of sensory input results in what has been termed the *retractable psyche*. This survival mechanism enables people to withdraw their consciousness in times of stress, so that only vital functions are present on the surface.[8] The vast and visible population, coupled with the basic human quest for identity, leads to the formation of *subcultures*. These allow for a type of tribalism and place of belonging, fulfilling deep-seated social needs.

The city also acts as a giant separating machine, intensifying socio-economic divisions which are present but more easily concealed in rural existence. Land values become an effective segregator of classes, as well as insulating the wealthy and powerful against incursion from undesirables. Thus *structural injustice* is often a cultural feature of urban life. The resultant tension contributes to the feelings of *alienation* and *vulnerability* which are experienced by many urbanites. People of every type and culture living in close proximity to one another produces *pluralism*, which deserves separate description.

PLURALISM

Pluralism refers to the close proximity of differing and sometimes competing belief systems, cultures and lifestyles. In pre-modern societies, there was a coherent and binding sense of what was right and wrong, how to live, what to believe. People did not have a developed view of cultures or religions – there was civilization and savages, orthodoxy and heresy. To a large extent this self-satisfied prejudice was

based on geographical isolation. Urbanization has elimi-
nated that luxury, and now Buddhists and Muslims, West
Indians and English, yuppies and homeless may all be
rubbing shoulders on the same tube carriage.

Pluralism easily becomes relativism. The popular form of
this is expressed in the attitude: 'You can believe (do, be)
whatever you like as long as it doesn't hurt me.' Relativism
seems to cast doubt on the whole concept of truth.[9] For this
reason, Christians become decidedly nervous in the presence
of such attitudes. They are standing on a tradition which
appears to claim for itself absolute and ultimate truth.
Relativism is the theological equivalent of a massive earth-
quake:

> And if, correspondingly, all faiths and world views are
> thus historical, relative to their stage and place in general
> history, how can any one of them claim our ultimate
> allegiance or promise an ultimate truth or an ultimate
> salvation?[10]

While antipathy to such a viewpoint might be understandable in Christian theologians, it is possible that we are over-
reacting, at least in the context of postmodernity. Certainly,
Christianity has a huge investment in the concept of truth,
but the nature of that investment needs to be clarified.
Postmodernity celebrates diversity. It is cynical of a concept
of truth which has been defined by a small group of 'experts'
(white male European academics), and used to dominate and
silence any other voices in the community. For too long they
have guarded the door to 'truth', and restricted it to an elite
group.

A new generation in a new culture want to throw the doors
open and listen to all the stories. If there is such a thing as
truth, they argue, it will emerge from listening to these
stories. The concept of truth they are reacting to is objective,
rationalistic, individualistic and linear. Stories, on the other
hand, are subjective, synthetic, relational and playful. Toul-

min notes a cultural shift in postmodernity from the written to the oral, from the universal to the particular, from the general to the local, and from the timeless to the timely.[11] This is a new way of accessing what is true (or 'real'), but it is not a discounting of the possibility.

The good news is that Christianity grew in a pluralistic context, and it did it by and large by telling a local, timely, particular story with an experiential slant. At the heart of our story is not a philosophy or a code of ethics, but a person. In the new environment there is an increased freedom for us to recount our story. It will not be the only one told, but if it has substance and authenticity, then that may well be communicated to the hearers.

HOLISM

Perhaps the major issue of Western conscience in recent decades has been that of the environment. Ecological disaster has come perilously close, and has served as a wake-up call to a previously complacent generation. In searching for the causes of the crisis, many commentators have turned their attention to the Enlightenment, and some to the influence of Christianity. Descartes' radical scepticism led him to make his own rational thought process the final arbiter of existence. This had the effect of setting humanity over against the natural environment, as well as introducing an individualistic and controlling element to human interaction with the world.

Such an attitude may have built on a Western Christian tradition which encouraged humanity to 'subdue' and 'have dominion over' the earth (Genesis 1.28). This utilitarian approach to nature has produced shocking ecological abuses. It has taken the communications revolution of the twentieth century to reveal exactly how much damage has been done. Recognition dawned rather belatedly that the only hope for the continued survival of the ecosystem of the planet was a change of attitude on the part of *Homo sapiens*. We have been forced to understand our dependence upon and interrelationship with the natural (or created) order.

The growing response in the emerging culture is toward holism and partnership. All living things, and even inanimate objects, are connected in a web of relationship. It is not possible to isolate elements of existence and treat them as if they had no bearing on the whole. The culmination of this is the resurgence of the 'Gaia hypothesis', in which the whole of the earth and all of its inhabitants and ecosystems are treated as one living organism. Whatever attitude may be taken to this, the concepts of *belonging*, *partnership*, *responsibility* and *relationship* are vitally important ones.

JUXTAPOSITION

A central and revealing metaphor of postmodernism is channel-surfing on television. When a person holds a remote control in their hand and flicks between a multitude of programmes, they are sampling reality. A whole range of subject materials presented in contrasting styles are processed simultaneously. An experienced channel-surfer is capable of watching three or four programmes at the same time, keeping enough of a narrative link to have some impressionistic grasp of the theme. Schooled on television and computer, new culture pilgrims cope easily with multiple realities which are juxtaposed.

Modernity thrives on linearity and systemization. Thought, speech and art need to have a logical if not temporal progression, with a beginning, middle and end. Postmodernism prefers juxtaposition, where many contrasting and even contradictory themes exist side by side at the same time. This allows intuitive leaps of meaning, and can serve to break open new insights.

The art forms and self-expression of the emerging culture are expressive of this sort of parallel processing. One of the favourite forms of postmodern visual art is that of collage, in which diverse materials are placed adjacent to one another. As Grenz describes it:

The goal of this tactic ... is to barrage the viewer with incongruous, even clashing images that call into question any sense of objective meaning.[12]

There is a great deal of *sampling* and *re-presenting* of material in unfamiliar contexts. An example of this is the film *Natural Born Killers*, in which a disturbing scene of sexual abuse is set to a sitcom soundtrack with canned applause. The impact of the scene is due to the incongruity of the two genres. In a world in which meaning has become elusive, the juxtaposition of stories or ideas may be capable of generating a way forward. In this aspect of its life, the emerging culture is engaging in play.

DESPAIR

The post-war baby-boomers were full of optimism. They may have rejected existing social conventions, but they did so with flowers, smiles, and unshakeable convictions that 'we can change the world', and 'all you need is love'. And why shouldn't they? The West was wealthy, there was plenty of work around, and it seemed that sex had just been discovered. The generation which followed encountered massive unemployment, economic rationalism, the nuclear shadow, and AIDS. The future, which had seemed open and promising to boomers, was filled with darkness and despair for Generation X.[13]

This darkness has overflowed into the formation of the emerging culture. There is an underlying sense of hopelessness and despair which colours much postmodern expression. After recording a track entitled 'Rape me' and an album with the working title of 'I hate myself and I want to die', Kurt Cobain blew his brains out with a shotgun. It was in many ways the logical expression of a life filled with confusion and pain, where significant relationships and rare achievements did nothing to fill the inner void.

The loss of a future which can be constructed and participated in has lasting effects on the way in which people structure their lives. The focus shifts very much to the present, with the emphasis on extracting as much enjoyment out of that sphere as possible, and damn the consequences. Witness the increase in smoking rates among young people, or the quasi-suicidal practice of refusing to use condoms in even casual sexual encounters. Self-destructive patterns of behaviour and the use of cynicism and black humour are symptoms of an underlying grief and despair for what has become of us.

The emerging culture is bleak about the future prospects of humanity. Self-mutilation, drug and alcohol abuse, high suicide rates, fascination with death, apoliticism; all are signs of a people without hope. Life is constructed not in planned and purposive response to an anticipated future, but in random and anarchistic hedonistic events. There is a connection here with the postmodern predilection for play. It would seem that the 'social fabric' is unravelling. But coupled with the despair is a hunger for authenticity; a desire for something 'real' enough to withstand the rigours of existence.

APOCALYPTIC

The loss of future often gives rise to a specific form of religious reaction, in the form of apocalyptic discourse. Apocalyptic literature, such as the book of Revelation in the Bible, is forged out of situations of powerlessness and hopelessness. The present order is so closed and oppressive that some cataclysm is predicted which will overthrow it, and hope is transferred to a point 'beyond the end'. Sometimes this results in bizarre behaviour designed to catalyse the time of tribulation, and bring about the culmination of the existing structures.

The emerging culture demonstrates apocalyptic tendencies in keeping with its sense of despair, but with a new twist. The end is foreseen, but without much prospect of hope beyond it. It may be that the influence of the nuclear nightmare coupled with millennial gloom has produced a distinctive form of apocalyptic. In his book *Life After God*, Douglas Coupland notes the prevalence of visions and dreams of nuclear destruction among his contemporaries.

> This flashing image is a recurring motif in both my everyday thoughts and in my dream life ... I look and see that the sun is growing too large too quickly, like a Jiffy pop popcorn foil dome, glowing orange, like an electric stove element. And then I am awake.[14]

Coupland, knowing that the immediate threat from nuclear weapons has diminished, argues that the ubiquitous visions of the end of the world may be the objectifying of a fear of nonexistence.[15] Whatever the cause, those who recognize the genre of apocalyptic will note its presence in diverse forms of contemporary culture.

HUMAN RELATING

In the absence of transcendent values or meanings, participants in the new culture are finding significance in friendship. Relationship is a very important word at the turn of the millennium. Partly as a reaction against the extreme individualism of modernism, partly as an act of desperation in troubled times, people have sought solace in each other. Not just in sexual or romantic couplings, but in a lively sense of community expressed among groups of friends. It is a new social tribalism among those who recognize in others something of their own experience.

In the nuclear families of modernism, each home had its own lounge room, often dominated by the television, where people shared physical presence and spiritual isolation. In the emerging culture, the lounges are the cafés, bars and clubs, where larger social groupings meet to share pain, companionship and stories. In a fragmented society, these groups function as pockets of resistance and renewal. If meaning and truth are to be found anywhere, they will be discovered in the context of community, where humanity is respected and accepted.

Some very new ways of relating have been initiated by the growth of computer technology. 'Virtual community' is now described as an emerging phenomenon among those with access to the Internet.[16] Email, the Web and discussion groups enable people who have never met to form relationships which are surprisingly vibrant and durable. Geography is no longer a barrier to the formation of intimate community. The important factor here is the sense of connection provided by Internet participation, and the underlying hunger which it satisfies.

TECHNOLOGY

The first enthusiasts for technology were irrepressibly modern. They were proponents of a pervasive and optimistic scientism, which assumed that applied knowledge could overcome all problems. The technological revolution has been carried through with overwhelming success in the West, despite some warnings as to the consequences.[17] To the average modernist techno-peasant, however, technology was regarded with a certain amount of reservation and suspicion. There was a concern that humans stay very much in control.

Postmodernists are children of technology. They embrace it enthusiastically for the enhancements it can bring to life. The emerging culture has a fondness for technology, and especially for its ability to increase the scope of 'play'. There is no longer any expectation that the technology is somehow going to solve existential angst, but it may well provide better ways of escaping from it. Channel-surfing, web-surfing, mixing sound and images in such extravaganzas as U2's *Zooropa* tour; it is all good clean fun which pushes back the boundaries of mortality, if only temporarily.

The preference in the new world is for 'soft' technology. 'Hard' technology is clunky, distant and somewhat unresponsive. Virtual reality, on the other hand, confuses the boundaries between external and internal. It is pushing back the frontiers, exploring new experiential territory. There have been recent arguments that drug use among the young is not so much 'abuse' as the employment of the ultimate soft technology.

> And, in fact, that is exactly what drugs are: a technology, but one which plugs directly into the chemistry of our own selves – the blurry side of things, about which we know the least.[18]

Drug use, on this view, is pioneering and exploratory. This is indeed a new world; whether it is brave or foolish remains to be seen.

TRUTH VS REALITY

Modernist Christianity, in keeping with modernist intellectual endeavour, is greatly interested in the truth. This is the fundamental reason for the existence of so many denominations, and the doctrinal debate which has driven several hundred years of definition and argument. Early creedal movements were narrative and fiduciary; those since the Reformation have been abstract and contentious. Truth is out there, and each group claims that it has the franchise on it. This form of religious belief could only have emerged within modernism, in which truth is objective, rational, dispassionate, coherent and Platonically eternal.

Postmodernists have given up on the 'game' of truth-seeking. They have recognized the not-too-subtle power dimensions involved in trying to define what is true. It is a smokescreen for deciding who's in and who's out, and who controls the game. There has been the growing recognition that every observer's experience is vitally affected by their point of reference. Consequently, if truth is out there, it is unknowable. The most we can speak of is 'my truth' and 'your truth'. While there may be some point in us swapping stories, it will not be in the expectation of attaining a 'meta-truth'.

The emerging culture is more interested in reality than truth. Reality has some connections with the existential category of 'authenticity'. What is meant by this is existence beyond hype, where there is consistency between word and action. Real people and real experiences are those which can be trusted in a world of charlatans and illusions. Correspondence with some external framework is not a factor in reality; in this way an experience on drugs may be 'real', while a lecture on thermodynamics is not.

IMMEDIACY

We have already discussed the future-deficient despair which is a mark of the new culture. Associated with it is a hunger for immediacy. Immediacy does not only refer to an impatience with waiting, though this is certainly a factor in the emerging world. Who would have thought that we could become restless waiting for fast food, or even more remarkably, tapping our fingers while waiting a few seconds for our computers to perform for us. The other, and more significant, aspect of immediacy is that of vitality; of a sense of connection with and involvement in present experience.

It was the lack of this which led Kurt Cobain to commit suicide. In the early days of undiscovered music-making, Cobain felt some exhilaration in the experience of musical performance, particularly in front of a crowd. Later, he found it hard to reach the intensity of feeling, despite being a superstar. His suicide note read: '... I don't have the passion anymore ...' The lack of direct intense participation in experience was enough to make him despair of life itself. If immediacy could no longer be attained, there was not much point in carrying on.

Postmodern culture is very much in-your-face; loud, fast and aggressive. It doesn't allow withdrawal to some secure buffer zone of reflection or analysis. The object is to be truly present and involved in the experience, whether it be sex or music. If necessary, drugs are a means of enhancing the intensity of the event. There is no preamble or post-mortem; the immediate present is sufficient in itself, detached from any wider network of meaning, value or interpretation. The only sin is that of judgement.

FAITH

In the death throes of modernism, the thesis was abroad that the West was entering a golden age of secularism, encapsulated by the slogan, 'God is dead.' Indeed, it seemed for a time as if scientific rationalism would succeed in excluding religious discourse as belonging to an earlier and primitive form of human development. In the face of this orthodoxy, the recent explosion of interest in spirituality has somewhat caught commentators by surprise.[19] The so-called 'New Age Movement' expresses a deep religious longing which is widespread and expansive.

Faith has become (if it ever ceased to be) an important part of the way in which people relate to the world around them. The 'dimension' of spirituality is experiencing a renaissance which would give the impression that it had been discovered for the first time.

> [A] dazzling and bewildering array of different spiritualities compete for attention, each of them claiming to be able to offer something that will help us find our souls again, and chart a safe course for the future. The goods on offer in this religious market-place range from messages from spirit guides and extra-terrestials, to neo-paganism, Celtic mythology and aboriginal spirituality – not to mention renewed interest in astrology and a vast range of psychological therapies offering the prospect of a renewed, holistic humanity.[20]

As Drane indicates, the spiritual revival has tended to be influenced by consumer culture, so that religious options are selected and combined to suit the tastes and lifestyles of their user.

Before Christians get too excited about the renewed interest in religion, however, it is well to note that the emerging culture's exploration of spirituality is in many ways a reaction *against* institutional Christianity as it has been experienced in the West.[21] The faith-full search for meaning is being conducted in an arena which is generally accepted as being post-Christian. Nevertheless, God is back on the agenda of the emerging culture, and there is an openness to a host of religious stories. Coupland again, in *Life After God*:

> Now – here is my secret: I tell it to you with an openness of heart that I doubt I shall ever achieve again, so I pray that you are in a quiet room as you hear these words. My secret is that I need God – that I am sick and can no longer make it alone. I need God to help me give, because I no longer seem to be capable of giving; to help me be kind, as I no longer seem capable of kindness; to help me love, as I seem beyond being able to love.[22]

It is possible that the story of Jesus may find a hearing once more, if it can be cleansed of its institutional accretions and retold in simplicity and honesty.

The Beckoning Finger of God

Religious fundamentalism, a strong force in the late twentieth century, would have us turn back from the future which has been impressionistically described above. It seems that we are entering strange and dangerous territory, and the pain of it creates a hunger for the familiar.

> They said to Moses, 'Was it because there were no graves in Egypt that you have taken us away to die in the wilderness? What have you done to us, bringing us out

of Egypt? Is this not the very thing we told you in Egypt, "Let us alone and let us serve the Egyptians"? For it would have been better for us to serve the Egyptians than to die in the wilderness.' (Exodus 14.11, 12)

In the history of the movement of God, there have always been those wanting to draw back and return to safety. But there has always been, at those same junctures, the beckoning finger of God:

Then the Lord said to Moses, 'Why do you cry out to me? Tell the Israelites to go forward.' (Exodus 14.15)

The postmodern world is certainly unfamiliar terrain. To those who stand on the cultural heritage of Western civilization, it can seem at times like a new invasion by the Barbarians. Perhaps it is unsurprising that many Christians perceive the emerging culture as the enemy, and look for ways to protect themselves against it. But faith requires risk, and the confrontation of danger. We may not be called upon to become citizens of the new land, but God asks that we at least enter it, and learn how to tell the abiding story of Jesus to its inhabitants.

8

Beyond the Boundaries

—

The new millennium is a time for irresponsible boldness. If the situation we face is extreme, then it may call for *praxis in extremis*. Peter, the focus of our reflections on Acts 10, was also the disciple who followed Jesus out onto the water (Matt 14.22–33). He learned in that experience that the call of the Lord may mean leaving behind safety and convention. He also discovered that the dangers which result are real, but that there is no reason to fear in the presence of Jesus. Perhaps this early lesson stood him in good stead when the time came to transgress his religious boundaries at Joppa and Caesarea.

The thesis of this book is that we face just such a fundamental juncture in the history of Western Christianity. While safety is a legitimate concern, it generally tends to militate against mission.[1] Perhaps once more Jesus stands outside the boat, as we huddle closer in the face of the storm. To go where he is requires stepping out of what is most familiar and into that which is self-evidently threatening and dangerous. This dawning age, patchily described in the previous chapter, is one which demands that risk be taken; that we exchange safety for discipleship and security for mission. For all its fearfulness, God is in our world.

The Spirit in the World

There is no doubt that the gift of the Spirit was given to the church (Acts 2.1–13), and that the Spirit was from the first intimately concerned with mission (John 20.21). It is fair to say, then, that the Spirit is at work within the church, prompting and goading toward reaching outward.[2] The church has at times regarded the Spirit as its private possession, to be guarded and enjoyed. One of the great disappointments of recent history is the way in which the Charismatic movement, with some notable exceptions, has focused on private experiential encounters, losing some-where along the way the thrust to mission.

A less appreciated aspect of the Spirit's work is in relation to the world.[3] The first few verses of Genesis have the Spirit hovering over the chaos as midwife of creation (Genesis 1.2). This is the opening scene in a drama in which God woos the whole created order. The Spirit, that dynamic forcefield of love surging from the heart of the Trinity, is the lure of God as Lover made present to the world. Much confusion has been caused in the minds of Christians by the so-called 'ethical' use of 'world' by John, which seems to suggest that the Spirit is divorced from the unsaved (John 14.17). But this is misleading. We have seen in Acts 10 that the Spirit is at work in the world well ahead of and independently from Peter.

One of the great discoveries of twentieth-century theology has been the *missio dei*.[4] This is the understanding that the mission of God precedes and creates the church. The church is invited to respond and participate, but it neither possesses nor controls mission.[5] The Spirit is at work in the world, drawing the world toward Christ; actively luring people who have no contact with the institutional church. I have met a man who came to faith when the sunlight shining through a hole in the curtain made the shape of a cross on the wall. This is the dance of the Spirit, creating life and hope in surprising places.

The vision and work of the Spirit is broader than the imaginations of the faithful. Because of this, mission always requires leaving behind the shelters of false religious ortho-doxy, and treading the virginal unexplored lands of dis-covery. It is painful and unsafe to do so. At certain points, like Peter on the rooftop, we will face crises where going forward seems to contradict what we have come from. The Spirit is justifiably compared to the wind. She is no respecter of our boundary markers. In the words of James K. Baxter:

Lord, Holy Spirit,
You blow like the wind in a thousand paddocks,
Inside and outside the fences,
You blow where you wish to blow.[6]

Us and Them

It is natural for groups and subcultures to form a sense of identity in distinction from outsiders. Those who study group dynamics know that the strength of that identity is affected by the quality of contacts the group has with the surrounding culture. Negative contacts greatly strengthen the cohesiveness of the group, while positive contacts weaken it. As the church becomes more and more marginalized within Western society, it has an inevitable tendency to see itself as existing in opposition to that culture. In order to bolster this important quality of self-identity, Christians build comprehensive subcultures to make them relatively independent of others.

The problem with this approach is that it is antithetical to mission. God is not only at work among 'us', but also among 'them'. If we cut ourselves off from contact with outsiders, we are excluding the sphere of the Spirit's most important work. In the purview of God's missioning work in the world, there is no 'us' and 'them'. The tendency to categorize people for the purposes of dismissal is the mistake of Pharisaical Judaism, as well as the blindness from which Peter and the early church needed healing. Many Christians exhibit fear of and separation from people who are different. Any responsibility toward others is seen in terms of evangelism: a tense and nerve-racked confrontation to be got through with as quickly as possible.[7]

Fortunately, God is still at work in the Western world. Often despite the church, people are drawn to the compelling story of Christ and the healing it offers. People who have no language to describe it find themselves experiencing God and having spiritual encounters. Like Cornelius, 'a

119

devout man who feared God', many participants in Western culture are followers of God by intuition rather than understanding. They have dreams, experiences, great searching questions. Many of them want to talk about them with anyone on the same wavelength. But it would never cross their minds that such discussion would take place in church.

Nor are they likely to gain much satisfaction from Christians in their workplace. The likelihood is that any conversation would be marked by guardedness, anxiety and confusion on the part of the follower of Christ. The contemporary Christian viewpoint seems to be that genuine spirituality is the prerogative of the church, and therefore any 'experiences' outside of that setting must be either false or evil. Not surprisingly, such an attitude does not engender trust or openness. New Agers, by comparison, are enthusiastic about embracing any expression of spirituality as contributing fresh raw material for their own pilgrimage.

Like Peter, we have to leave our place of security and travel to where people are living and pursuing questions of meaning, if we are to witness the work of God. This involves dropping our 'them' and 'us' categories, and greeting people as equals and fellow spiritual pilgrims. When we do, we have the joy of discovering and continuing to learn what it is that God is doing in our changing world. Mission, for us as for Peter, is a two-way street. To go with the expectation of having all the answers for other people's questions is a form of arrogance. It is among 'them' that we learn who God is, and why they remain a part of 'us'.

Crossing Boundaries

A year or so ago I had an interesting experience. On a Sunday night, we had celebrated worship as Parallel Universe, an alternative worship venture which I have been involved with for the last four years.[8] After packing out, the worship planners retired to a central city bar and café to celebrate, unwind and debrief. Unknown to us, it was the anniversary of the particular establishment's opening, and they were having a party. The place was packed, but we found a table and ordered refreshments. There were people of every type in the place, it being one of the only bars in the city open at that time on a Sunday night.

While we were enjoying the festive atmosphere, three transvestites dressed in blue-sequined splendour climbed up onto the bar. They were gorgeous, made up to the full and pouting. Conversations died down, music started on the sound system, and these three began their act. They lip-synched and performed a synchronized dance routine to 'I Will Follow Him' from the film *Sister Act*. The crowd loved it, and clapped and cheered wildly. In the midst of this risqué entertainment, I felt the unmistakeable presence of the Holy Spirit. It caught me by surprise because it was so unexpected. But I had no doubts that that was who it was.

On any conventional Christian interpretation, this event should not have happened. God is not supposed to show up in bars where transvestites are performing. To this day I am uncertain of the significance of the event, other than that God was somehow present and rejoicing in the midst of a very human celebration. It served to remind me once again that God will be where God will be, and those who object to it are on shaky ground. Many Christians would not have gone near such a bar in the first place. I think I understand why they come to such a position. But only those who were willing to enter the door got to experience that simple but profound visit of God.

All of us have boundaries. If the venue had been a pornographic cinema or a strip club then I would not have crossed the threshold either. We know when we are approaching our boundaries because of the degree of internal stress which is generated. This is occasioned by leaving behind our comfort zones, and entering territory which is unfamiliar and threatening. We are aware that this is terrain where we do not know the rules or the language, and that creates anxiety. There is a deep-seated human instinct to back off from boundaries, and often for very good reason.

On the other hand, we have seen in Chapter 5 that Jesus was an inveterate crosser of boundaries, and that God often calls us to follow him into new realms. The dilemma is often created by the way in which we view boundaries. It depends whether we have a focus on 'leaving behind' or 'crossing into'. If we feel that we are leaving behind those things which are essential to our identity and well-being, then we will be rightly reluctant to transgress boundaries. If, on the other hand, we see them as borders of a new and exciting land, we will be keen to get on into the novelty of the unexplored.

For the Christian, the courage to cross boundaries must come in certainty of the resurrection, and a deep assurance that nothing 'in all creation, will be able to separate us from the love of God in Christ Jesus our Lord' (Romans 8.39).[9] Our conviction is that there is no territory or future which is not already included in the salvation of Christ. Therefore we can cross all frontiers, including that of death itself, in the certainty that God is ahead of us. And where God is, there is no reason to fear. This is no guarantee of immunity from harm, as the history of mission demonstrates. But it should be sufficient to provide confidence and authority for our mission endeavours.

The entire history of Christian mission might be described as the progressive crossing of boundaries. At each juncture, it seemed that potential loss outweighed potential gain, and yet in retrospect it is clear that obedience required courage and determination to proceed. Many of the boundaries crossed thus far have been geographical, social or cultural. Those which confront the church most immediately are those of gender discrimination and sexual orientation. No doubt there will be more in the future which are as yet unseen. In all of them, we will be nervously exploring unseen territory in partnership with a restless God.

The Humanization of the Church

It is time that the Western church woke from its death-like sleep and began to grieve for its lapse into irrelevance. We have succeeded in separating Christ from people, so that they imagine he is the icon of good and respectable people, and has little relevance to their own sordid and tangled lives. Jesus who lived and died as a 'friend of sinners' has been blasphemously translated into the enemy and judge of sinners. The grace and forgiveness which he offered has been swallowed up by self-righteous and prudish moral crusading. The healing love of God is once more locked up in sanctuaries and ceremonies.

Sectarian drift has allowed the church to become a private club with high entry requirements; one that is seen as a burden on the backs of ordinary people rather than a sign of hope. Outside the walls of the church, people are literally dying without anyone to represent for them the God of our Lord Jesus Christ. In order to be reconciled once again to the work of God in the world, the church must reorient itself to the sphere where people go about their daily lives. Because the church has become inhuman, the task before it is one of humanization.

The church is inhuman not in the sense of self-consciously setting out to oppress people, though some victims of clergy sexual abuse could be forgiven for thinking so. The church is inhuman in the dual sense of being cut off from the humanity of its own members, and being absent from the mass of humanity outside its doors. Both of these failings grow from an unconscious theological heresy: the denial of the full humanity of Jesus. In Protestantism, the sign of this heresy (docetism) is the empty cross adorning church buildings, from which the body of Jesus has been removed. When the human Jesus, who also brings the fullness of God, is allowed to return to the Gospels, then the church can begin its journey of humanization.

THE HUMANITY OF JESUS

Christians struggle to believe in the humanity of Jesus in the same way that the very first disciples struggled to believe in his divinity. For them there could hardly be any doubt as to his humanity.[10] They had eaten and joked with him, smelled his sweat and seen his blood, felt the warmth of his embrace and the lash of his tongue. He spoke as someone special, and they knew that he was marked out by God. It took many years after the resurrection to sort out the deeper significance of his life, until they finally stumbled across the wonder of the incarnation.

Western Christians peering back through two thousand years of interpretation have the opposite problem. Jesus is for them the risen Christ, Lord of all creation. He is seated at the right hand of God, and at his name every knee shall bow. While contemporary believers acknowledge that he lived on earth, the image they hold of Jesus never quite touches the ground. The sort of humanity we ascribe to him is very different from our own.

The gospels give ample evidence of the humanity of Jesus. We see him angry (Matthew 21.12–17), tired (Mark 3; 9, 10), grieving (John 11.35, 36) and in despair (Luke 22.41–6). The great confession of the book of Hebrews is:

> For we do not have a high priest who is unable to sympathize with our weaknesses, but we have one who in every respect has been tested as we are, yet without sin. Let us therefore approach the throne of grace with boldness, so that we may receive mercy and find grace to help in time of need. (Hebrews 4.15, 16)

This passage is enormously important in understanding the necessity of holding fast to Jesus' humanity. Without it, we have no hope of salvation for our own. The direct link is made here between Jesus' full participation in humanity, and our own hope of mercy and grace.[11]

While the docetic divinization and ethereal disembodiment of Jesus springs from noble motives, it is difficult to imagine a more damaging blow to his accessibility. In his own ministry, Jesus was available to the crowds through his presence. An interpretation which lifts him out of the human arena cuts him off from that point of contact. A God who is not present to or involved in the angst of human existence may be admirable, but is of no real help, and has no right to speak. If Jesus is not our brother, then neither can he be our saviour.[12]

OUR OWN HUMANITY

The direct result of exalting Jesus out of his humanity is the development of a faith which is in itself inhuman. When our efforts at discipleship are guided by a false image of the one we are following, then we find ourselves striving for unrealistic goals. Western Christianity has inherited a Hellenistic streak of disdain for embodied existence. When this comes to flower in an untenable theology of holiness (as outlined in Chapter 5), it results in a thin, bloodless and supercilious faith. Believers are urged into aspirations and commitments which are unliveable. They are spurred on by bizarre stories of heroes of the faith.

Many Christians are ill at ease with their own humanity. This can be illustrated by attitudes to two universals of human existence: suffering and sin. Suffering is the central human reality. It is the one experience guaranteed for humanity – an authentic mark of human living. To deny suffering is to deny humanity.[13] Jesus Christ, the centre of Christian life, suffered on our behalf. He suffered in his compassion for his friends and the great crowds of lost people; he suffered a sense of abandonment by those same friends and even God; he suffered the despair of approaching death; and he suffered massive physical pain in his crucifixion.

One of his earliest and most passionate followers wears his affliction and suffering as a badge, and is able to admit that at one time in ministry 'we were so utterly, unbearably crushed that we despaired of life itself' (2 Corinthians 1.8). It is difficult to understand how one of the most central themes of Christianity – the dignity and hope of human suffering – could be neglected almost to the point of extinction in some circles.

The denial of suffering blocks the well-spring of human passion. When people do not give recognition or permission to the pain of inevitable tragedy, they create a shallow and deceptive centre to their lives. The attempt to live in stoical indifference to life's measures of loss, betrayal and brutality creates people who have no credibility or authenticity. They exclude themselves from the fellowship of suffering, and are thereby disenfranchised from comment. Christians need to accept their own pain, and allow and be available to others who are hurting.

When it comes to sin, the same orchestrated denial seems to operate in many sections of the church. The acknowledgement of sin, and a means to end its power, are concepts which are again central to historic Christian faith. The much misunderstood doctrine of original sin is a way of admitting to the universality of sin in human existence. In noting that we continually fall short, Scott Peck notes:

> Christianity allows for that. In fact the one prerequisite for membership in the true Christian church is that you be a sinner. If you do not think you are a sinner, you are not a candidate for the church.[14]

And yet the fallacy continues to be abroad in Christian circles that sinners are those who are outside the church.

This error in judgement has profound consequences. A deep appreciation of one's own participation in sin is a prerequisite for experiencing and valuing grace. The biblical affirmation is that we are free from the power of sin in Christ, not free from its reality. Once again, cutting ourselves off from our own deep sinfulness has the effect of distancing us from our humanity. The temptation of the

Pharisee in the Temple appeals to us (Luke 18.10–14): to imagine that we are not sinners, and that we consequently may have pity on those who are.

A healthy sense of sin keeps alive the profound amazement that the grace of God in Christ continues to suffice to keep us on the Way. It also builds bridges between ourselves and those who have not yet encountered grace. We gain a sense of identity with them as fellow sinners. If we have anything to share it is a sense of hope for our common predicament. Because of this, we come to others as fellow travellers, rather than as those who used to be like them, but have now moved on. The self-congratulation of any kind of convert is ultimately patronizing and distancing.

MAKING THE CHURCH HUMAN

When the members of the church participate fully in their own humanity, perhaps they will lose their fear of engagement with the humanity of others. The challenge of the next millennium lies in the humanization of the church. Its task is to make the drama of Christ present in the world of commerce and cohabitation. The evidence of its success will be when the human drama makes its presence felt within the life and worship of the church. When there are tears and laughter alongside ritual and prayer and singing, then we will know that Jesus is once more in the world.

One of the most underrated expressions of Christian mission in the twentieth century has been the chaplaincy movement. Shop-floors, workshops, staff rooms, hospital wards, offices and prison cells have experienced the presence of representative Christian persons. In many cases, such chaplains have gone into new situations where they are stripped of the privileges and emblems which usually accompany ministry. Without pulpit or prayer-stool, they have been forced to begin with the simple strategy of building friendships with people they have never met. This has generated a fair amount of brokenness among chaplains, which may well be the secret of their success.

127

Through this sort of ministry, church is made present in diverse settings and for people who might otherwise have nothing to do with Christianity. Chaplaincy is thus an expression of humanization for the church, as well as being an innovative model of mission. The question which must be asked, however, is why it is necessary to have especially designated and commissioned people to be 'chaplains' in the world? In almost all of the settings where chaplains work, there are already Christians present. How are we to resource people to be natural Christ-carriers in whatever sphere of influence they occupy? It is clear that a reorientation is needed before they can be effective as missionaries.

Perhaps the sign of the church's humanity will be when Christians can relax at parties and pray in pubs. Or when they can talk about their episodes of depression with a non-Christian workmate. If Jesus is making a difference in the journey of life, then there is no need to hide anything or pretend to be any more or less than who we are. A cup of coffee or even a shared cigarette can be every bit as sacramental as a communion chalice, when it carries the love of Christ. Humanity is our shared gift from God, and when redeemed by Christ, can be an offering which carries hope and grace to those who receive it.

Presence As Mission

God is deeply involved in and aching for the lives of people who have traditionally been written off as beyond the pale by the church. In modern cities, the place to go prospecting for the presence of God is in psychiatric wards, methadone clinics, twelve-step programmes and boarding houses. Here where people's veneer of competence has been shattered, it does not take long for discussion to turn to what we would recognize as 'religious' topics. But even among those who give a better show of having their lives together, there are moments of growth and transition when they are reaching out for meaning.

The simple but profound strategy of mission, as recounted in Acts 10, is to be around when God is doing things. This means being present, in every sense of the word. Certainly it means being physically present in the furnace of life where people love, grieve and search. But even more than this, it is necessary to be emotionally and spiritually present; to have the status and role of a friend. Only then can we point out the activity of the Spirit, and share that little bit of grace and light which has penetrated our own hearts. Mission is nothing but partnership with God, witnessing the unfolding story of Christ.

The world of the future as described in the previous chapter is uncharted territory. Even those who welcome it and celebrate the passing of the old order are unsure of what the new era will mean. The institution of the church in the West is unlikely to survive the transition without major reformation. It could easily slide further into isolated insignificance. Those prepared to cross the border and explore the unknown will have to possess the mission-orientation and risk-taking courage of Acts 10. They will need to go where the people go, and make sense of the purposes of God from a new location.

New challenges call for new responses, and once again the tradition needs to be mined to see what it can produce to point the way forward. Reformation is a job similar to building a new structure on existing foundations. It requires demolition so that the foundations can be rediscovered. But it also demands that the process of rebuilding occurs. It is to that more positive agenda that the next few chapters turn.

9

Spirituality for the Times

—

Spirituality is booming in the emerging culture. The eruption of interest in spirituality has caught erudite secularists by surprise. As John Drane notes:

> Suddenly, it's trendy to be spiritual ... what was once regarded as a minority interest – the preserve of idealists who patronized wholefood shops, burned joss sticks and read the works of eastern mystics – has now become big business. It is fashionable to be Green and spiritual.[1]

In the midst of this revival of interest in the spiritual, the Western Protestant church appears more arid and barren than ever. Several centuries of romance with the Enlightenment have left many streams of the church devoid of mystery, magic and meaning.

More germane to our discussion, however, is the need for a spirituality which will not simply sustain people, but empower them for the task of mission. If, as has been suggested, mission involves living beyond the borders in strange and difficult territory, then it is vital to survival that relevant resources are found to support and engender such mission. Spirituality in partnership with mission cannot be static or defensive. It must be dynamic, open, embracing and engaging. Above all it must be genuine; it must be able to co-exist with the ambiguous and unsettling experiences of life outside the walls.

A new situation for the church will require a new spirituality. Urban missiologist John U'Ren acknowledges that 'to undertake ministry at "the coal face of the frontier" requires a special integrity, openness and honesty'.[2] The greatest danger facing mission practitioners in recent times has been burn-out. Many people who have suffered this condition report the depletion of inner resources as external demand outstrips their inner capacity. The spiritual traditions which they have inherited have proved inadequate to refresh or nurture them in their place of encounter with the world. Crisis forces them to search for new sources of encouragement.

A Spirituality for Mission

What is needed is the forging of a new and vibrant spirituality which is adequate to the call to mission in the new millennium. While drawing from the deep wells of Christian tradition, this spirituality will need to be responsive to engagement with contemporary Western culture. It will be a missionary spirituality, in terms of promoting and maintaining the divine journey toward the other. If it is to be adequate to this task, it will need to be *earthed, conversant with human suffering, attainable within the complexities of life, holistic, creative, communal* and *contextual*. While there may be many expressions of such spirituality, they will need to contain many of these qualities.

EARTHED

Too much Christian spirituality contains the Hellenistic dualism of body/spirit, with body being regarded as inferior and limiting, while spirit is noble and uplifting. The result is a spirituality which is disembodied, disengaged and ill at ease with normal human existence. The glorious creation story of Genesis 2.4b–25 contains a rich image for the understanding of humanity. In creating humans, this account pictures God reaching down and scooping up a handful of earth, and then breathing the divine breath/life into it to give life. Humanity is viewed as an amalgam of mud and the breath of God, joined so as to be incapable of separation.

A spirituality for the third millennium will need to lose its discomfort with sexuality, embodiment and the apparent scandal of God's incarnational working. It will need to find both the spirituality of physical life, and the physicality of spiritual expression. Earthiness is a prime indicator for saints, and a sign of acceptance of God's blessing of humanity. Those who engage in mission will have their feet planted firmly on the good earth, for they recognize it both as something God-given, and as a common resource with the whole body of humanity. In their own lives they will accept and celebrate embodied life, making it a means of appreciation for the good gift of God.

CONVERSANT WITH HUMAN SUFFERING

As already reported, the experience of suffering has become a process of separation of Christians from the wider population. There is, especially in some sections of Evangelicalism, a strangulated denial of suffering. Any form of spirituality which cannot look suffering full in the face and give account of itself, is not worthy of the title Christian.

The starting-point for a renewed spirituality will be a recognition that human existence entails suffering, much of it meaningless and without value. There can be no denial of the horrors of rape, suicide, disease, starvation, psychiatric disorder, homelessness or divorce. Nor can there be the suggestion that faith in God will protect anyone from the incursion of suffering, or the more blasphemous suggestion that God causes or at least willingly permits such ravages. The message of the gospel, however, offers the possibility of dignity and hope within suffering by suggesting that even seemingly pointless suffering can be redeemed by God. Any new spirituality will be based around the Christian image of a God who suffers with us and for us.

ATTAINABLE WITHIN THE COMPLEXITIES OF LIFE

Modern urban existence is extraordinarily stressful and complex. Henri Nouwen speaks of 'the restlessness, the loneliness, and the tension' which is engendered by 'this hectic, pressured, competitive, exhausting context'.[3] Many proffered approaches to spirituality take no cognizance of this situation, and rely on patterns of discipline and retreat which are the legacy of simpler agrarian worlds. While they have some useful contributions, the consequence in the life of believers can be one of guilt and frustration. It seems that the only possibility of spiritual life is one of abnegation and asceticism, admirable from a distance, but inaccessible to the majority of city dwellers.

Spiritualities of withdrawal and isolation are not helpful to the current task of mission, which requires engagement and participation. The vast majority of images used in Christian spirituality are rural, and therefore do not immediately connect with urbanites. A criterion of any valid spirituality for the West must be that it is possible and attainable within the given world. It must be constructed out of and valid within the experiences and demands of urban technological life. Such an approach to the spiritual life will necessarily look and feel different from traditional models.

HOLISTIC

Life is already split and fragmented, and many people feel the lack of a sustaining centre to existence.[4] A spirituality adequate to the missiological task will be one which is integrating and holistic. In the development of New Testament Christology, the drama of the Christ-event reaches cosmological proportions (Colossians 1.15–20, Ephesians 1.3–14). In doing so it binds together creation and redemption so that the purposes of God and the meaning of human existence are united. Contemporary Christian spirituality will need to rediscover this emphasis, and move toward bringing together disparate elements of faith and experience.

Today the separation between the human race and the realm of nature is keenly felt. The ecological crisis not only represents a structural or organizational problem; it is also an expression of alienation which people experience from the organic world. As Fox and others have noted, the emphasis on redemption in some sections of the church has been at the cost of creation, creating a split which has been lethal to the environment.[5] This needs to be overcome. Today there is a hunger for *connectedness* and *belonging*, whether in relation to nature or to other people. There are spiritual resources to address this quest within the Christian tradition, but they need to be made available.

CREATIVE

Postmodernity represents in part a volcanic uprising of those aspects of human life which have been suppressed by modernism. Creativity is one of the gifts of God to humanity, whereby we share in the ongoing creative work in the universe. It is both a resource for and consequence of fertile spirituality.

Art has a long history of association with Christianity, and for many centuries the church was the supporting locus of art and artists within society. Since the Enlightenment, however, art has been disparaged and artists forced into exile by the church. A sign of renewal within the Western church would be the return of artists and their work to dialogue with the community of faith. Christian spirituality is capable of enriching and releasing the creative endeavours of not only artists, but all who find relationship with God the Creator. Such creativity has the power to inspire and communicate with people at levels other than that of the spoken word.

COMMUNAL

Western existence in the late twentieth century bears the wounds of a deeply-rooted individualism which has left people isolated and alone:

Loneliness is one of the most universal sources of human suffering today ... Children, adolescents, adults, and old people are in growing degree exposed to the contagious disease of loneliness in a world in which a competitive individualism tries to reconcile itself with a culture that speaks about togetherness ...[6]

Whatever spirituality of mission is developed will need to draw on the Christian tradition of communality, and oppose and subvert the reign of the individual. It cannot be the exclusive domain of the individual pilgrim, but must be resourced, expressed and celebrated in the context of community.

A spirituality forged in community will give up on the attempt to carry the full burden and responsibility of Christian life as an individual. It will be interdependent, meaning that there will be times when we rely on others to carry us and times when we will be the carriers. We will be free to contribute whatever it is we have within us, confident that there will be others who will provide to compensate for our deficiencies. A Christian communal spirituality will reassure us that our lives are shared with others rather than being our exclusive domain, and that we have a place of belonging which transcends geography and culture.

CONTEXTUAL

In the land where I live, Christmas cards picture horse-drawn sleighs sliding over frozen wastes. Shops decorate their windows with frostings of holly and mock snow. The irony of this lies in the fact that the Antipodean Christmas falls a few days after the summer solstice. With the sun beating down, native trees flowering and beaches beckoning, many New Zealanders insist on providing a roast meal followed by Christmas pudding. The whole performance is out of place in the southern hemisphere, as is the celebration of resurrection at the onset of autumn. It is an example of the way in which Christianity has failed to be transplanted into local culture, and remains foreign and distant.

If a spirituality is to 'work', it needs to resonate with the experiential world of the participants. The symbols and language of the spirituality have to be vernacular, in that they are owned and understood. Christian mission has always understood the need to translate Scripture so that the many peoples of the world may hear in their own language. But neither the permission nor the impetus to translate spirituality has been so readily forthcoming. In order to nurture inner resources, it must be possible for the heart to find voice in its interaction with the Christian story.

Resources for Spirituality

Within Western Christianity, there are various legitimate resources for spirituality which have been strip-mined, and are consequently running close to depletion. Sources such as prayer and Scripture are legitimate in themselves, but taken in isolation from any other tributaries become strained and barren. If a broader and more mission-oriented spirituality is to be nurtured, it will certainly draw on a range of resources, some of them non-traditional. Some of these are explored below, starting with the more orthodox ones before surveying the less well appreciated.

PRAYER

Prayer within the Evangelical tradition tends to be relatively simple and straightforward. It is talking to God, either inside one's head or out loud. There are various modes of praying, such as thanksgiving, petition and intercession. But the methodology of prayer is doggedly verbal. In essence it is a one-way communication, from petitioner to God. While such an understanding of prayer has sufficed for many, over time it can come to seem unbearably trite and dull. It is difficult to sustain a one-way conversation with anyone, and the feeling of being somewhat foolish as one's words bounce back from the ceiling is difficult to dismiss.

The contemplative tradition enriches the understanding of prayer. Now prayer is understood as waiting before God, and may include the discipline of silence as well as the recitation of liturgical material. The emphasis here is on meditation, quietness, receptivity and devotion. This attitude to prayer 'requires that we stand in God's presence with open hands, naked and vulnerable'.[7] There is a degree of intimacy with God, and the analogy to prayer which is developed in mystical literature is that of sexual relationship. This type of praying is at once more mysterious, engaging and renewing.

However, if the danger of petitioning prayer is that of a thinly veiled pragmatism, the danger of contemplative prayer is that of quietism. The need is for a form of prayer which combines both *depth* and *responsive action*. God must be encountered in the public sphere as well as the private sphere, and the two must inform each other. The forms of prayer are hugely varied: lighting candles, using a kneeler, repeating the 'Jesus prayer', writing prayers in reflective mode, taking intentional devotional walks through the community, praying with media such as clay or paint, conducting public prayer as protest, singing or chanting prayer, and of course the essence of all prayer – silence before God.

SCRIPTURE/STORY

After a couple of centuries of applying intellect to Scripture in various forms of 'criticism', it is time to allow the Bible to be what in essence it always has been: a collection of stories. Listening to or reading stories is not primarily an application of intellect. It is an act of shared imagination. In story, one is invited (not coerced) into a different world through the use of active imagining. Neither is the process one-way. Whoever encounters a story brings with them their own story, and on creative ground the two are allowed to interact and cross-fertilize.[8] This form of communication produces encounter, and encounter may lead to change.

How then to apply imagination to Scripture in a fruitful way? Sermons, which constitute the bulk of Protestants' encounter with the Bible, can be depressingly rational and dull. This is the legacy of the 'expositional' school of preaching, which is astonishingly intellectual. Sermons also epitomize one-way communication. There are other ways of coming at the Bible. It can be acted out, read in parts, or discussed in groups. People can be invited to use their imagination to 'feel' their way into Gospel stories. Alternatively, people could be asked to share something of their own story, and then think about how Scripture has any relevance to it. If there has to be a sermon, there could be discussion afterwards. It is imperative that Scripture be set free for its subversive task.

PARTYING/CELEBRATION

Jesus was a great one for parties. From the scene of his first miracle (John 2.1–12) to his many discourses around the dinner table (Luke 7.36–50; Mark 7.1–23), Jesus' social life is such that he is looked down upon by the religious people for his indiscriminate and gregarious behaviour. The culmination of history in the kingdom of God is portrayed as one big party (Luke 14.15–24). The sheer festivity of the messianic movement is one of its most attractive features.[9] Disembodied Christian spirituality and an undue emphasis on the ascetic has given the impression that partying is the antithesis of spiritual formation, but this is in denial of the tradition.

Certainly celebration in denial of life is unchristian: where the aim is to escape and get 'out of it' so that the pain of existence may be temporarily suspended. But followers of Christ will be able to celebrate with enthusiasm in the face of life, without denial of suffering or ambiguity. The cause of celebration is the hope and freedom won through resurrection; the effect of such celebration is to extend hope and freedom within the proximate world. The test of vital faith may well be the ability to enjoy oneself dancing.

Celebration of any sort, whether in joy or grief, is constructive of spirituality. It deepens appreciation of God's good gift of life, and shares the burden of private pain with others. Moreover, celebration is open, participative and accessible in ways that few other activities are. Common meals (in their natural form, not the stylized form of the eucharist) are abundant sources of spiritual enrichment. There is something quasi-mystical about the joining of people in eating and drinking, linked together by the common table.

RISK-TAKING/BOUNDARY-CROSSING

We have in the previous chapter emphasized the importance of crossing boundaries for the sake of mission. There are few people for whom this comes naturally, and without large amounts of anxiety. The capacity for taking risks or crossing boundaries is something that needs to be worked at and prepared for, like running a marathon. There is a strong psychological and spiritual inertia which sets in at mid-life, if it has not already, that makes people more unwilling to experience genuine risk.

One of the preconditions for reckless endangerment of personal safety is faith in the ubiquitous presence of God. Like Peter climbing out of the boat, we need to incrementally test ourselves against the idea. Crossing boundaries requires practice. None of us find it easy to live without the approval and understanding of people we respect. And yet crossing boundaries means relinquishing much of that affirmation. Like troops on the front line, it becomes important to develop good lines of supply. It is important to have a few friends who share the same vision and are rock-solid in their support. Reading the Gospels becomes essential, and learning how to search for and find Christ in the stranger. Regular time out for reflection helps to maintain sanity. But the danger is worth it, for it is beyond the margins that God is most clearly at work.

TRANSPARENCY/VULNERABILITY

Amidst the predominantly functional relationships of the

city, there are great pressures on our inner resources. In order to survive and protect relationships, we build fortifications around the most tender parts of our psyches, and place them off-limits to the majority of people. We don't want the masses trampling over our sacred ground, and rightly so. However, this results in our presenting masks or personas to the outside world in order to function. Once having adopted a strategy of presenting faces to people, it is easy to use it in the wrong circumstances, and to begin to lose perception of who we truly are. This is not good for spiritual development.

The only counter to this threatening loss of identity is unnatural candour. As Frederick Buechner tells it:

> It is important to tell at least from time to time the secret of who we truly and fully are – even if we tell it only to ourselves – because otherwise we run the risk of losing track of who we are truly and fully and little by little come to accept instead the highly edited version which we put forth in hope that the world will find it more acceptable than the real thing.[10]

With transparency comes vulnerability. When we are honest in a context where others are not, it seemingly gives them an unfair advantage over us. Some will use it to ridicule or denounce us. But others will find in our disarming honesty the freedom and encouragement to be honest about themselves.

HUMOUR/CYNICISM

Paradoxically, running in the opposite direction from what has just been said, is the need to survive in the city. The great task of Christian life is discernment; knowing when to be open and when to stand back. Jesus' injunction to 'be as wise as serpents and innocent as doves' (Matthew 10.16) seems apposite. Both humour and cynicism are mechanisms for survival among people who suffer. Humour is a human expression of transcendence: the ability to stand outside of a situation in order to lovingly ridicule it. Like all gifts it can be misused, but in its best form humour is full of human poignancy.

Laughter, when it is not mocking or derisory, is wonderfully therapeutic. It is renewing and refreshing, and even in times of tragedy can be the key to unblocking wellsprings of spiritual energy. It is astonishing how often in the context of a death, family members will end up laughing at times until their tears of joy mingle with their tears of pain. It is a good thing to laugh in the face of death. What is the resurrection, other than God's greatest joke? You either get it or you don't.

Cynicism is a more dangerous resource. It can easily become a corrosive acid which dissolves everything good in life. People operating on the margins are susceptible to cynicism, and if not handled with care, this can lead to the ugly child of bitterness. On the other hand, a judicious use of cynicism may be a way of affirming the inherent sinfulness of humanity, and thus be a better guide to realism in spiritual life than credulity.

SELF-EXPRESSION/PLAY

Fear of rejection pushes people into hiding their gifts from public sight. It seems that our culture of competition and success inhibits creative self-expression amongst all but the most talented. But failing to express what is within one is the equivalent of blocking the outlet of a pond; it becomes stagnant and foul. Self-expression, whether in art, writing, music, sculpting, flower-arranging or cooking, is a means of participating in the life of God. It is letting be; bringing to fruition that which was not, and has come to life only through the expression of our imagination and practical skills. In part at least, this is what we were made for. There is great excitement and satisfaction in self-expression, whether or not it is appreciated by others.

Play is sometimes frowned on in Christian circles. It is seen as the domain of children; something that mature people grow out of. This is simply not true. Adults retain a capacity for play which allows enjoyable sexual frolicking and relational game-playing among other things. We of the church are in danger of being too mature for our own good. There is a great need to lighten up and enjoy life, and to rediscover the sensations of wonder and awe. The call is not to be childish but child-like in our approach to life. Absorption in play is a spiritual resource; a means by which the false world of commerce and status is treated with contempt in the light of the kingdom.

PROTEST/SUBVERSION

The values and priorities of the Way are quite different from those of the surrounding culture. Particularly in the techno-cratic and economically obsessed West, it is inevitable that followers of Jesus will run into conflict with the powers-that-be.[11] In order to affirm their faith, and to be disciples, Christians must inevitably protest.

There are three guidelines for Christian protest. Firstly, it needs to take place in the public arena, in the same way that Jesus challenged local power structures at the Temple (Mark 11.15–19). This involves confrontation and the willingness to bear the consequences. Secondly, it should not expect to be successful even if sometimes it is. The call is to faithful-ness rather than success. Our job is not to bring in the kingdom but to bear witness to it. Thirdly, it should express creativity and life. Too much protest cannot think outside of demonstrations and petitions. We have a rich and inspiring prophetic tradition of dramatic protest on which to draw.

Subversion is a subtler form of the same resistance. It involves refusing to play by the rules or adopt the priorities which society decrees as normal. The Christian movement has always been powerfully subversive in acknowledging an authority which lies outside the bounds of existing powers. To use the words of Peter: 'We must obey God rather than any human authority' (Acts 5.29). Opting out of consumer-ism, treating one's career lightly, standing alongside the marginalized; these are acts of both subversion and spiritual formation.

WORSHIP/AWE

Although worship has been left till last, it is one of the most important spiritual resources available. Much worship in the West tends toward the tedious. If God is not bored with it, then many church members are. It fails to inspire or engage the imagination. Even in Charismatic churches, it can be verbose, cerebral and patronizing. For increasing numbers of Christians, worship is an experience of oppression rather than liberation. They have turned aside in despair, making their protest through non-attendance, and struggling to keep the stuttering flame of faith alive in isolation.

Some, however, have sought to recapture worship as something which leaps wet and wild from the bog of captivated hearts; which stretches convention until it rips and allows God in; which draws words and symbols from the raw experience of participants and flings them to God in love and desperation. Some have shared their discoveries in a loose network known as the 'alternative worship' or 'new worship' movement. In gifted moments, they have found God yearning and wooing in their midst in such a way that it seems possible to hope for a future for the church again.

There are of course many other sources of spirituality than those surveyed here. When the heart is captivated by Christ, then all of existence becomes a resource for growing in depth and understanding. There need be no rigid compartmentalizing of life into sacred and profane areas. The promise of Scripture is that Christ is within us, and that the Spirit is at work in the world. We need not be fearful or anxious, but can relax and enjoy travelling in partnership with the One in Three. For Christians, spirituality is nothing other than participation in the life of God; and God is available at all times and places.

10

Finding Faith

In the story from Dunblane which John Drane recounts in Chapter 2, he asks some perceptive questions in response to his experience.

> In recent years I have gradually been moving towards the conclusion that our words are getting in the way of the gospel – that the church is somehow imprisoned in a kind of cognitive captivity which is inhibiting our mission, maybe even keeping Christ on the fringes. What would our evangelization need to look like to break out of that bondage? And what would our churches need to be like to create a space to accept and encourage the growth of the kind of spirituality I met that night on a cold pavement in Dunblane?

We have thus far addressed the issue of spirituality. This chapter and the next will respectively look at evangelization and the church, in terms of the demands of mission in the new millennium.

One of the major problems with conversion is that two thousand years of church history have left the impression that we know what it is. That very familiarity, bordering on arrogance in some circles, clouds the picture when it comes to the sort of reinterpretation necessary because of the church's current crisis. Most discussion on evangelism focuses on technique and strategy; the mechanics of salvation. This assumes that the problem is simply one of communication – that somehow or other the message (which is static) is not getting through, and therefore we need to adopt new methods of conveying it.

Unfortunately, the crisis is much deeper than this. In the post-Christian era, the medium is the message, and the medium of evangelism is regarded with extreme distaste by the surrounding culture. There are, of course, certain historical touchstones of the gospel which will remain determinative, and we cannot dispose of them simply because they become unfashionable. But both Scripture and the history of the church give us permission and encouragement toward the presentation of faith in a variety of ways which are appropriate to our context. The apostle Paul is a fine example of one who was able to translate the mysteries of Jewish messianic expectation into concepts familiar to a vastly different set of hearers.

We must allow our own tradition to speak to us radically, and respond to it in the context of our own culture. If this is allowed to happen, then we may discover that the story of Jesus once more offers us a way forward.

Followers of Jesus

Many contemporary notions of evangelism betray their modernist and rationalist origins. Faith in Christ has often been reduced to assent to a set of propositions. Evangelism easily becomes a marketing ploy for Christianity, akin to selling encyclopedias. Various techniques are used in a highly manipulative agenda designed to get prospective customers to 'sign up'. This is about as far away from the story of Jesus of Nazareth as it possible to get.

The first followers of Jesus had very little idea of what they were getting into at all. Going by the Gospel stories, it is hard to understand what motivated them to leave behind their secure environments and follow a stranger. We can be certain of only a few things. The initiative lay with Jesus rather than the disciples, in itself a reversal of Jewish custom.[1] Second, the disciples responded to an invitation to follow, without much detail as to their destination or even the nature of their journey.[2] Third, they could not stay where they were and still follow this invitation.

But invitations have to be accepted, boats have to be

145

abandoned and other responsibilities ignored (Matthew 8.20–2; Luke 9.59–61).[3]

Fourth, the first companions of Jesus did not come from among religious or respectable people. Instead, they were from among what Gill describes as 'little people' and 'notorious sinners'.[4]

Jesus does not seem to have employed a very effective screening programme in the selection of his disciples. He does not ask them for a statement of belief or even commitment to a programme of action. Nor does he appear to take much interest in their moral life. The invitation is simply to accompany him as he moves on. To contemporary ecclesiastical ears, Jesus' invitation sounds irresponsible and vague. And although church history has shaped the tradition to highlight the role of the twelve disciples, it is apparent that the followers of Jesus were a much wider and more fluid group, including women (Mark 15.40, 41).

It was over the course of Jesus' travels in Palestine, 'along the way', that his followers began to get some understanding of what he and his movement were about. There were the healings and miracles which attracted the huge crowds (John 6.2). The provision of food also proved to be a powerful magnet for the multitudes, so much so that Jesus had to direct their attention to the real significance of his work (John 6.25–34). Gradually, as the messianic procession moved along, the closest friends of Jesus began to get an insight into where this was all heading, and they were not keen on the final destination (Matthew 16.21–3).

The closer they got to Jerusalem, and the denouement of the journey, the more the followers of Jesus slipped quietly away. By the time they arrived at Golgotha, there were only a handful left, standing at a distance (Matthew 27.55). Some of his dearest friends, including Peter, had deserted him. At what stage of the three-year journey do we determine who were the followers of Jesus? Was it the hangers-on looking for entertainment and free food? Or was it the faithful who lasted the distance and watched in horror as he died? Of course even that is not the end of the story, as the resurrected Jesus rehabilitates a drop-out such as Peter (John 21.15–19).

At what stage did they cease being observers of the movement, and become participants? It is not at all clear. Perhaps we can say of those who became so captivated by the dream of Jesus and his kingdom, and devoted the rest of their lives to his name and his cause, that they were truly followers of Jesus. Looking back, these survivors might say that the transformation they had undergone in following this man was so profound as to represent a kind of rebirth. They might have had more difficulty responding to the common Evangelical question of the day on which they were born again.

Who's In/Who's Out

The propositional ambience of conversion has more to do with the boundaries of the institutional church than it does with biblical discipleship. For some time now, since the Reformation at least, the church has had an inappropriate concern with determining who's in and who's out. Prior to that time, the context of Christendom meant that citizenship and Christian faith were regarded as coterminous. To deviate from the faith was to warrant anathema in such a way that exclusion from the social and political community followed. Heresy was a civil offence. In this climate, it is assumed that everyone (apart from a few deviants) is in, and so membership is not much of an issue.

The Reformation created a crisis, in splitting the church into several streams. Now which stream one was in became critical. The Reformed churches by necessity defined themselves in opposition to the Catholic church which they had rejected. The distinctive features of their difference were codified into doctrinal statements which became credal. One belonged by affirming the central principles of polemic identity. The symbiosis of faith and citizenship was by and large maintained, however, by rearranging political reality to match the new denominational map.

It was the Radical Reformation which brought the relationship between church and state under scrutiny. The so-called Anabaptists made baptism a matter of faith, not citizenship, and so challenged the religio-political power structure. They determined to follow Jesus in disregard of state law, and many paid the consequence of martyrdom. In their emphasis on discipleship as the only true sign of faith, the Anabaptists recaptured something of the biblical emphasis on following Jesus.[5] Their strong emphasis on mission led them to call people to follow Jesus by leaving their previous life and adopting a new way of living.

The Radicals therefore managed to break the Christendom alliance of faith and civic duty, restoring Christianity to its original status of conflict with the existing powers. However, their concern for who was a 'true' Christian lead them to develop an ecclesiology of the 'gathered' church; that is, the church as a community of those who were truly saved. They defined themselves over against what they regarded as lax churches, where infant baptism included people who self-evidently were not in a position to make a decision about following Jesus.

Since the Reformation, then, all streams of the church have been concerned with membership. In a context of denominational plurality, it became vital to know who belonged and who didn't; who were the insiders and who the outsiders. Whether allegiance was to credal statements (as per the historic Protestant churches) or to the magisterium (as per the Catholic church) or to the community of the truly saved (as per the Free church), group identity and boundaries took on new importance. Belonging to a particular church in distinction from others overshadowed the commonality of being followers of Jesus together.

It is against this backdrop that conversion has been interpreted. While all give lip service to the wider significance of finding faith in Christ, denominational allegiances have shifted attention to who's in and who's out of a particular brand of Christian church. Boundaries have become important, and entry requirements are of course carefully laid down. Conversion has subtly become entwined with church membership, necessitating its control by the various institutional hierarchies.

Membership and boundaries are legitimate institutional concerns. All corporate legal identities have means of identifying their members. But the kingdom of God is not an institution. Hence the question of who's in and who's out of the kingdom is not easily defined. In the parable of the wheat and the weeds (Matthew 13.24–30), Jesus cautions against any attempt to separate the good from the bad, the 'saved' from the 'unsaved':

> But he replied, 'No; for in gathering the weeds you would uproot the wheat along with them. Let both of them grow together until the harvest ...' (Matthew 13.29, 30)

The kingdom is not only compared to a field containing both wheat and weeds, but also to a net which contains all kinds of fish, both good and bad (Matthew 13.47–50). The emphasis in both parables is on the eschatological locus of judgement, suggesting the futility of prior attempts to achieve this.

Jesus' teaching on the kingdom indicates the hiddenness and ambiguity of it. Like yeast in dough (Matthew 13.33), it is not always apparent where the boundaries are on this side of history. The attempt to determine or define insiders and outsiders is misguided, because the 'first will be last' (Mark 10.31) and 'whoever is not against us is for us' (Mark 9.40). It is therefore not within the responsibility of the church to determine who is saved and who is not.

People determine for themselves their allegiance to or rejection of the kingdom. Along the way, they position themselves either closer to or further away from the movement of Jesus. Such movement is not always evident from the outside. Presumably this is why judgement is the prerogative of God. Conversion is more of a process than an event, which is understandable once it is accepted that the kingdom of God is a movement rather than a club. Words (even confessions of faith) are less important than active participation (Matthew 7.21–7).

What implications does this have for the church? Is there a role for the church in relation to the kingdom of God? Thankfully, yes. The church is both the first fruits of the kingdom and a sign of the kingdom. It is the dynamic community created by God's mission in Jesus to the world, the band of travellers alert to and following on the Way. It is also a rough pointer to the life of the kingdom, so that it can be experienced rather than talked about.

An Open Community

An emphasis on membership and mode of entry has given some sections of the church a hard boundary. It is extremely difficult for outsiders to gain access, whether for theological or cultural reasons. The usual institutional factors of hierarchy, control, regulation and sanction come into play. Were the church to continue in this mode, it would be destined for oblivion in the West. If conversion is regarded as a process, and identity governed by participation rather than doctrine, then a very different model of church becomes possible. Church is then an open community of people who are endeavouring to help each other along the Way.

For some years now the congregation I belong to has adopted a slogan to describe its ethos: 'open at the edges, committed at the core'. The thinking behind this has been to remove all obstacles to people moving into the community. In this sense the congregation has been radically open. People are welcomed whatever their background, whatever their dress, whatever their language, whatever their sexual orientation, whatever their theology. Whatever reasons people turn up for, their dignity is accepted. For a long time we had a Welsh agnostic, who would make full use of the 'free-for-all' time in worship to ask hard questions and dispute the claims of Christianity.

The philosophy behind this structure is based on the power of attraction rather than compulsion. If Christian life is even partially what is claimed of it, then the hope is that it will have a magnetic power to it. The quality of life and community displayed by the core disciples is intended to draw those who look on from the edges. As people move toward this core, they begin to learn progressively some of the responsibilities and commitments of following Jesus. As much as possible, a seamless transition is provided from the edges to the core. If there is any boundary point, it is in the affirmation of baptism.

One of the discoveries of this group of people on the Way together, is that the experience of community is in itself powerfully evangelistic. In a world starved of relationships, it seems that even the most basic functions of community life are powerfully attractive. In those special times when the congregation is able to achieve honesty among participants and before God, there is a qualitative experience of *koinōnia* which seems to penetrate defence mechanisms. It is not the kingdom of God, but in these precious moments the community becomes a sign of the kingdom which Jesus promised.

Of course, an open community is subject to misunderstanding. Christian onlookers may decide that it has no standards or genuine faith. Newcomers might interpret the lack of pressure upon them as a sign that nobody is concerned for them. People with no inclinations toward faith may come and abuse the hospitality. Core members can feel disappointed that they don't have more status as insiders. But it is worth it all for the ease with which unchurched people of every type can find acceptance and a relational guide to the real presence of the risen Christ.

Community exists only when persons really know each other. God as love is experienced not in large organizations and institutions but in communities in which people can embrace each other.[6]

Journey Toward, Journey Away

Dave Andrews,[7] founder of the Waiters' Union in Brisbane Australia, has used mathematical terminology to discuss the difference between existing models of conversion and church, and a more helpful paradigm to carry us into the next millennium. Andrews suggests that our institutional paradigms of church operate much like the mathematical concept of closed sets.[8] The sets contain groupings of members, who constitute a set because of their distinction from those who are not part of the set. Naturally, the set is defined by a fixed border. Any-thing or -one outside the border does not belong to the set; any-thing or -one inside the border is a member of it.

Andrews proposes a different 'open set' model. Open sets do not have boundaries, but are defined in relation to a centre. Adapting this approach to the kingdom, Andrews suggests that we accept Jesus as the centre of the set. Rather than concentrating on who's in and who's out of the set, attention can be paid to those moving towards the centre and those moving away from it. On this model, all is not as it seems. People who are members of the institutional church in the conventional sense may very well be moving away from Jesus. On the other hand, people who have no formal relationship with the church might be moving towards Jesus, and hence be included in the set.

Such a model is at once more dynamic and ambiguous. It emphasizes journey, faithfulness and movement in a way which recalls the Gospel stories of Jesus' trek toward Jerusalem. The harsh line between Christians and the community is removed, without diminishing the importance of relationship to Jesus. It is the overall progress of a person's life which is of importance, rather than one isolated incident. Decision remains important, but it is an ongoing choosing which is determinative, and actions are every bit as illustrative of such deciding as are words.

None of this is intended to dissolve the concept of church into some romantic concept of the 'invisible church'. Within history, church only happens in the context of real people who can be seen and touched and argued with. Church is an approximation of the kingdom, and will always be the carrier of the dark side of humanity as well as the light of grace. The kingdom is broader, deeper and richer than the church. But would-be participants in the kingdom find themselves inevitably relating to and through various physical representations of the body of Christ. There is no escape into utopia.

The Way

Following Jesus has implications for the way in which people live. Travelling toward the Carpenter of Nazareth results in changed lifestyles. This is the message of Jesus, the message of Scripture, the message of the Anabaptists, and the message of Bonhoeffer.[9] Cheap grace is neither attractive nor satisfying. Unfortunately the paradigm of conversion and church life offered in the twentieth century West pretends to offer salvation with not much more than a change of opinion.

Too often, we have conceived of salvation – what God does to us in Jesus – as a purely personal decision, or a matter of finally getting our heads straight on basic beliefs, or of having some inner feelings of righteousness about ourselves and God, or of having our social attitudes readjusted.[10]

Against such a background, genuine discipleship may appear fanatical and subversive. Metz describes it as 'class treason'

– 'a betrayal of affluence, of the family, and of our customary way of life'.[11]

When one considers that Jesus had very little to say about sexuality, and a great deal to say about money and possessions, it may be argued with some validity that the contemporary church has lost sight of Jesus and is following some other agenda. The man from Nazareth had strong opinions about family and the place of it in the scheme of things; most of this teaching being antithetical to current Christian viewpoints. Those who followed Jesus originally gave up much in the way of security and comfort, but did it because they had found something better. Present-day followers are like a man who found a treasure in a field, and went home to sit in comfort and talk about it.

The lack of courage in resisting cultural pressure is due in large measure to failures in worship and community. Many congregations unwittingly provide divine encouragement and blessing for the unbiblical lives we are living. Such worship is comforting, but of little help if the comfort it offers is false. The God who is represented as winking at materialism and promoting middle-class values is not the God of Jesus Christ. A Christian community must be a community *of Christ*; one which coheres around the crucified saviour. Moltmann identifies this man as a rebel and a blasphemer, whose challenge to societal values resulted in his death.[12] A Christian community, then, will be a community of resistance.

Individualism is both a substantive and a methodological challenge to discipleship. Cultural values are so powerful and pervasive that it is not possible for individuals to mount an effective resistance to them. Either they will be regarded as harmless eccentrics, or they will succumb to cumulative and persistent pressure to conform. It is very difficult, for example, for a person in a worshipping congregation to adopt a lifestyle of voluntary simplicity, when all around are fellow Christians happily pursuing a life of consumerism, without apology or regret.

It would, on the other hand, be possible for a congregation

to begin together a tentative journey of exploration of the teachings of Jesus on wealth and possession. This could be accompanied by a corporate pledge for people to help and encourage one another to find ways of putting such teaching into action in their own environment. But congregations do not generally operate as Christian communities. They are instead gatherings of individuals. Each individual or grouping within the church determines their own affairs, which may be reported to others, but certainly not with any expectation of sharing the decision making process.

Storytelling

Truth in the Christian context is not propositional. Because of its locus in Jesus Christ, it is always personal. The means of communication favoured by Jesus, endorsed by Scripture, and largely forgotten by the church, is that of storytelling. Storytelling is open and participative. It does not impose itself upon hearers, but invites them to take their own imaginative stance within the structure of the story.

> When we preach sermons, or hand on ready-made summaries of Christian belief and theology, we inevitably present ourselves as experts. Doing it that way, it is all but impossible to avoid giving the impression that we are people who have it all together, people with no questions. But when we tell stories, we reveal ourselves as weak and vulnerable – spiritual pilgrims with whom others can identify.[13]

Jesus' explanation of his own parabolic teaching highlights this point: 'The reason I speak to them in parables is that "seeing they do not perceive, and hearing they do not listen, nor do they understand" ' (Matthew 13.13). This may not be a programme of deliberate deception as some have interpreted it, so much as a recognition of the way in which stories function. Stories lead but do not compel;

they beckon but do not berate. In the culture of post-modernity, story is the vernacular.[14] It is the means of accessing the culture, and missionaries must be fluent in it if they are to have any hope of communicating.

Take, for example, the following story. God, it seems, is closer to sinners than to saints. The reason is this. God wants to hold on to every person on the earth, and does so by means of a long string. Whenever somebody does something wrong or hurtful, however, it has the effect of cutting the string, and the connection is broken. If this happens, God has no choice but to tie a knot in the piece of string. If it happens over and over again, a series of knots is needed to effect repair. Each knot makes the string a little shorter, and draws the person on it closer to God. That is why sinners are closer to God than saints.

Now it would be possible to analyse this story, to find its meaning, to debate the theological issues it raises. But that would be precisely to negate the story and disempower it, by the application of modernist techniques. The desired response is to listen to the story, to ponder and to smile, to feel the tension and protest it creates. In this way we begin to interact with the story, by bringing to it our own stories, and in turn being led forward in the progress of God's story. Stories do their own work – they do not require interpreters. This is the fundamental self-understanding of the gospel in historic Christianity.

The responsibility of Christians is to continue to tell the story of Jesus, both in their living and in their words. If it is what we claim it to be, then it will remain attractive and powerful in continuing to call disciples. If not, then we can appeal to absolutes and the authority of Scripture until we are blue in the face, but to little avail. Our world is weary of sermons, but hungry for stories. Those who walk the path of the gospel will have plenty of raw material, both from the tradition we have inherited, and from our own experience along the Way. But only if we are travelling it.

11

Models to Hope On

-

Criticizing the Western church is relatively easy. What is desperately needed is a way ahead. As described in Chapter 6, it is vital to establish transitional structures to implement new and hopeful modes of being the church. While the faithful can experience grief at the impotence of the church, they cannot stay in grinding despair without becoming utterly hopeless. They cry out for some form of reasonable response which they can make, some change which they can participate in.

What is required are models of alternative church life. Models go beyond theory, in that they can be touched and observed and participated in. My own involvement in Parallel Universe (described below) has given me insight into just how important a function alternative expressions of faith can be. Time and again we have seen people energized and brimming with hope after participating in a worship event, simply because they have understood that it is possible to break open the boundaries in a way which is still faithful to God. Many have gone back to their own contexts to experiment and play, thus multiplying creativity.

It is important that the deep critique of this book be matched by some suggestions of a way ahead, and that these suggestions be grounded in functioning communities. In choosing to describe some models, however, caution is needed. To portray a community in words is not the same as participating in the reality of that community. Something which sounds very fine in words can be guilty of obscuring the frailties and defects of the all-too-human reality. None of the ventures described here would want to make any grandiose claims about having found the answer. They are all rather small struggling ventures which count survival an achievement.

However, I have chosen to describe local models which I have some knowledge and experience of, so that their veracity and integrity can be supported. New Zealand is a highly unchurched society, and so in some ways at the leading edge of post-Christian experience.[1] The following models are all very different from each other. They represent one of the central convictions I have regarding the future of faith communities: there is no one model to be pursued. What is required is a creative and multiform approach to reforming the church which keeps faith with its own context and community. The purpose of these models is to inspire others to attempt their own, not to come looking for a pattern to copy.

Where possible, I have invited participants in the following ventures to provide descriptions, and so the perspectives are those of insiders. The limitations of space mean that there is probably as much hidden about each of the models as is revealed. Nevertheless, the five communities described offer hope for the future of the church in the Western environment.

Parallel Universe

Parallel Universe grew from the dreaming of Mark Pierson, urban minister and current pastor of Cityside Baptist Church in Auckland. He had friendships with people in the 'alternative worship' scene in the UK, and had been inspired to try something different in the New Zealand context. He pulled together a team of four people, including himself, as a leadership and creative energy think tank. Parallel Universe has been running now for four years. The most public part of its life is the monthly worship event. A visitor describes it as follows:

On the outside, this place looks like any Auckland night club might. In fact it is a night club, the Powerstation, venue for many touring bands. Walking in I catch a hint

158

of the fumes left from last night's rock concert. Inside, there is ambience, atmosphere. Chairs are arranged around tables, café style. Rock music plays over the sound system. There's a bar. Homegrown art surrounds the three video screens on the walls.[2]

The byline of Parallel Universe is 'Worship that's off (and on) the wall'. It is a loose community of people who seek to create worship for themselves and their peers which is relevant, creative and open. The stated aim of Parallel Universe is to build a community within which people who have given up on the church or their Christian faith can be 're-faithed'. At the same time it is conscious of those who have never had any encounter with Christianity at all. As founder Mark Pierson puts it:

Parallel Universe is not a reaction against the church. It isn't anti-church. It isn't a stepping stone to the church. It seeks to be a community of people drawn together to worship and serve and to extend the Kingdom of God. It *is* church.

While newcomers are sometimes dazzled by the multi-media approach to worship, the heart of Parallel Universe is something deeper and more subtle. Pierson says 'Our desire has always been to try to discern something of what is going on in our rapidly changing post-modern culture, and to work at forms of expression of the Christian faith that are relevant in that culture.'

Worship services are participative, multi-sensory and multi-linear; they weave in and out of a particular topic, but not necessarily in any systematic fashion. Bible verses will be flashed on the wall at the same time as some relevant video is screening, with a music track pounding in the background. There are no designated leaders, and no recognized 'front' to the worship. Anything can, and does, happen. There have been huge gas flames rising from the ground, bottles of Chardonnay descending from above, vigorous responsive prayers, live bands with lots of dancing, banquets, compressed air nail-guns, prayer walls for people to scribble on, candles and incense, and the miracle of the meat pies and beer. Always the worship environment is created and styled to suit the nature of the event; sometimes with angels and upside down Christmas trees, others with rocks and palm trees.

The worship is often based around a theme of some sort; titles have included 'Re:incarnation', 'Fire in the Dark', 'Bad to the Bone', 'Why Worry?' and 'Why is an Instrument of Torture Hanging Out in Madonna's Cleavage?' In addition to the monthly worship events, Parallel Universe has other low-key meetings on intervening Sunday nights. There is a community night, an issues discussion night, and the Quiet Service, which is a simple contemplative communion service. Formal structure is almost non-existent, with a highly relational community resisting institutionalization. Parallel Universe is constantly changing and evolving – more of a movement than a place. Many people from both within the church and outside of it have found in Parallel Universe a sign of hope.

Graceway

It was the energy of Steve and Lynne Taylor which gave birth to Graceway in the suburb of Ellerslie in Auckland. In the midst of pursuing a theological education, they felt the need to flesh out their dreams in attempting to plant a new type of church. Steve has provided the following description of the result.

Creative; real; honest; relaxed; relational. These are the core values that make and shape Graceway. We have been described as 'appropriately different'. We intend that worship emerge from the community through interaction and feedback. So we write, draw, share, reflect on images, sing and pray. It's a lot like Forrest Gump's box of chocolates; you are never sure what you'll get. That is part of the creativity. We're committed to flushing the religious equivalent of artificial stimulants down the toilet, so our worship starts from the space people are in and attempts to interact with the real world.

An essential part of this is the 'bar stool'. If you cruise down to Ellerslie's local pub, you'll sit on a bar stool, catch up with your mates, bitch about work and discuss life. The Graceway bar stool has a similar role, as a focal point where people can be honest with the community. We've celebrated new births and a child's first pair of jeans, got angry at an unjust dismissal, shared the heartbreak of the death of a three-month-old baby with congenital heart disease and discussed films and books. The bar stool always finishes with a prayer for what is shared and our world. I guess that's a big difference between Graceway and the Ellerslie local.

We try to love God with all of our minds, so we still have a 'sermon'. Ten to fifteen minutes when we work hard to connect with a visually-oriented age. Scripture is the ground of our being and the guide to our lives. Yet we reckon that for too long it has been approached like the Emperor's new clothes. So we're trying to ask Scripture our honest questions. We're also committed to modern educational understandings and so the 'sermons' use a range of communication methods that help people learn for themselves.

We're committed to mission that respects the fact that evangelism is a process and involves saving more than the soul. We work at hanging out one on one with people on the margins. We fly a 'Snoopy and the Red Baron' float in the local Santa Parade, give out free water with John 4.13, 14 written on it and show films like *Lion King* at cheap rates for struggling families. We ran an Easter programme called 'The Original Rolling Stone' when the Rolling Stones came to town at Easter. Just trying to make connections for unchurched people.

The bean counters always want to know about numbers. We started with a committed team of eight in September 1994. We now average eighteen to services, with a committed group of about thirty. A third of these were religiously disenfranchized or completely unchurched prior to coming to Graceway. We are lawyers, machine operators, scientists, solo caregivers, shop assistants and welders.

We enact the belief that the Holy Spirit is active in our world. So we listen to our society's poets and singers and watch the work of our filmmakers. They seem so much closer to the heartbeat of humanity. Marketplace resources are used in our worship and we work at cooperating with what God is doing in people's life journeys. We are part of the Baptist family of churches and appreciate this wider family's mission focus, commitment to Scripture and freedom at a local church level. However, we also seek a more inclusive ecclesiology, to utilize traditional resources, and attempt to keep grace, not legalism, at our core. Why the name, Graceway? The content says it all. We seek to be a place of grace.

Spine

The Urban Youth Mission Project (known affectionately as 'Spine' by its participants) grew from the gifts and vision of a person. Simon Chaplin, and his wife Anet, had been working from a church base in Christchurch for some years. Simon was Associate Minister, with special responsibility for youth. He both discipled young people from within the congregation, and formed relationships among alienated youth who were a long way from church of any kind. His heart was for these angry, broken and perceptive young adults who were crying out in protest against a lifeless culture.

A project was initiated which envisaged inner-city Auckland youth culture as a mission field. Funding was cobbled together, and Simon and Anet, complete with three children, called as pioneer missionaries. Simon was given complete freedom to make contact with youth culture however he thought best, and to search for God. His work was in dialogue with a Field Team.

Most of Simon's work takes place at night, and mostly on the streets. He tells the story of a typical encounter, this one with Eddie, a male sex worker who Simon has befriended.

It was one o'clock in the morning. I was asleep, the phone rang. It was Eddie in tears. He'd been beaten and robbed – not badly beaten – just a broken foot – but broken; he was broken on the inside – a broken spirit! Within five minutes I had him in the hospital. Over the next four hours we yarned, cried and laughed. About his childhood abuse, his ugly lifestyle and God.

There's a beautiful and simple movement of God on the street, and when social service is street level and relational, you are privileged with seeing the gospel and Jesus work in someone's life ... Our conversations drifted, with Eddie saying things like, 'Why, if God knows every hair on my body, am I like I am?' – 'Why can't I get a handle on God and live like him?' – 'I mean Simon, why has he placed you in my life and world; I want to die.' Inside of the sex workers' community I witness and receive real love, care and comradeship – these are pockets of God in their culture.[3]

After more than a year on the streets, Simon and Anet have established a small community in the heart of Karangahape Road, the notorious centre of the sex industry in Auckland. There in two adjoining flats, anything from six to twenty adults live with a collection of children. Also, young people have found accommodation nearby and are part of the fledgling group. There are no 'services'; just meetings where the community comes together to eat, talk and pray. They have dreams – a café, accommodation, a worshipping community. For the meantime they are content to be in touch with God, the street, and each other.

Reflecting on his experience, Simon challenges:

> In the final analysis the big question isn't how do we re-engage with our world or how do we become relevant again ... rather, do we want to? ... If the answer is yes, then the process will be to ask: 'What is God already doing in the emerging generation; what are the pockets of God in our culture; and how can I facilitate people to experience God, his grace and salvation; and what are the relevant forms of spirituality/church/culture and change!'[4]

Spine is a sign of hope amongst a generation that doesn't have much of it. It is still finding its way in uncharted territory. But Simon, spearheading the mission, is constantly discovering the presence of God in places which have been regarded by the church as God-forsaken. 'There is a spirituality on the street, almost asking to be interpreted ... We need to interpret [it], to declare the ultimate hope and love, belonging and meaning in life, through the God able to be known.'[5]

Bread and Breakfast

The following evocative report comes from Andrew Dallaston, participant and occasional scribe for this lively group.

> It's ten to nine on a Sunday morning, and as usual our family's running late. In theory Bread and Breakfast starts at 9.00 a.m. every second Sunday, but most of us drift in any time up to about 9.45 a.m. This week the group's meeting at Alex and Rosemary's place. We move around the various houses that are big enough to hold us in reasonable comfort. The adults also meet in home groups one evening every fortnight.

The pot luck meal is in full swing as we arrive – a variety of cereals, fresh fruit, muffins, croissants, real coffee – best breakfast of the week. The kids pick and play while the adults stand around, eating and chatting, catching up on what's been happening in our lives. This time is essential. By ten(ish) when the more organized portion of the morning begins there is no ice to be broken. We are friends, family, meeting together in a relaxed, informal, natural atmosphere. About 22 adults and 15 kids are packed into the living room, about average for our Sunday gathering.

We begin with a bit of singing accompanied by piano and guitar – new songs from photocopied sheets, with thoughtful lyrics. Now the person leading for that morning presents a short all-age segment. Occasionally we may call in a guest speaker, but the group has an amazing depth of talented people including two ordained ministers.

The family dog decides to try religion and joins us ... tail wagging hopefully. She is excommunicated. Another song to settle us down and we take communion. We read a short, simple liturgy together, prepared by members of the group. Two slices of wholemeal bread are passed around ...

'May the body of Christ feed and change you.'

Two simple silver goblets of a rather nice port are sent on their way ...

'May the blood of Christ make you whole.'

A Beethoven concerto plays quietly in the background. Cicadas and birds sing outside. The words of one of our songs run through my mind.

Not in the dark of buildings confining,
not in some heaven, light years away,
but here on this earth the new light is shining,
now is the kingdom, now is the day.

I look around at the kids and the adults and feel at home. This is a good, life-filled place to be.

165

The kids head off for a game of softball. Most Sundays it's some form of Christian education, a craft activity or perhaps rehearsing for a play. Usually the adults would have some meatier input followed by discussion, sometimes breaking into smaller groups to make sharing at depth even easier or perhaps a time of meditative worship. This week we're talking about general directions for the year. Community building seems to be one theme that emerges, deepening our commitment to God and each other.

At the end of this session we might finish with a short prayer or more likely another song, then it's on to general business. One of the refugee families we support needs some help with school fees and uniforms. A Somalian woman is trying to raise airfares to bring family to New Zealand. Their situation is dangerous, the need urgent. We all readily agree to supply the $3,000 she needs; part gift, part loan. Some of the group give regularly, others donate to specific requests, but there is no pressure because there are no regular expenses, no leader to pay or building to support, and without hierarchy we can respond immediately rather than taking the matter to committee.

There is enough real friendship and trust in the group that we can be open about our doubts and problems, our hopes and dreams. We are free from pews, suits, structures and conforming expectations, free to journey where God leads us as individuals and as a community. And if we often take the scenic route ... I say hallelujah!

Glenbrook Community Church

Simon Brown and his wife Anita have been pivotal in the formation of Glenbrook Community Church, a congregation in a largely rural area south of Auckland. Simon is bivocational; working part-time for the church and earning money by building for the rest. Glenbrook meets in a

166

hockey-club bar, and has conducted many experiments in creative worship with the use of appropriate symbols (incense, rocks, marshmallows, preserved fruit and Renaissance art), drama, video, drawing, etc.

The community works hard at acceptance, seeking to provide an environment where everyone can feel welcome: 'There needs to be common respect for each other, and space for each person to say their piece in a safe environment.' At the same time, the primary focus of worship services is that of encouraging and renewing the followers of Christ, rather than outsiders. The format of such services is relaxed and participatory. Simon describes the philosophy of the church as follows:

At Glenbrook we have endeavoured to explore what it means to be a radically biblical family church. Our model is taken from a healthy Christian family sitting around a table enjoying a meal together. At the family dinner there is laughter, anger, schoolkids, mess, prayer, noise, discussion, communication, excitement, correction, silence, food, infants, etc. Realistically, we expect no different at family worship. Consistent with our model of family at the table, we don't have Sunday School or crèche during the worship service. We stay together and worship God as whole families. In order for this to work the service needs to be short and varied. The format runs something like this. We have an introductory activity, brought by one family; a singing slot or communion; someone is rostered to bring a four-minute devotion. We have a barstool time and a fifteen-minute sermon. The whole service takes an hour with a drink and bikky break at half-time for the kids. We finish the whole thing with a shared meal.

Members of the community participate in an annual covenanting to one another, which has to be opted into or out of each year. It involves a commitment to Christ and to the community, as well as to personal spiritual development.

Although Simon is well aware of the risks of legalism involved in such covenanting, he firmly believes that 'there can be no true community or fellowship without unswerving commitment'. The high expectation at the centre accompanies encouragement to develop a broad approach to life. No person in the community (including the pastor) is required to attend more than two meetings per week. The church closes down for six weeks over the summer holiday period, allowing people to relax and meet informally, and to prepare themselves spiritually for the new year.

The community has a strong sense of mission, viewing the congregation as a mission headquarters. Within this philosophy, every community member is considered a missionary in their own right. 'Our hope is that the love of Christ will be spread across boundary fences wherever the believers go, and that opportunities to proclaim the Gospel of Jesus Christ will follow,' says Simon. 'No rush though,' he adds. Simon believes that worship is a potent means of evangelism, and that the worship of the community is powerfully attractive.

Indicators

What are we to make of these very different approaches to church and mission? Not, certainly, that they have found the definitive answers. One of the commonalities among each of these groups is that they see themselves as being on a journey of discovery. Answers are few and far between, but they report learnings along the way. They also share a dissatisfaction with contemporary forms of the established church, and have made a determined attempt to move beyond existing models. As a result, there is an atmosphere of vitality and passion in their activities, which is powerfully attractive. Slowly, cautiously and in unorthodox fashion, outsiders are coming to faith in Christ through these communities.

Perhaps, on the basis of their stories and those of other

experimental groups, it is possible to suggest some indicators from the journey into unexplored territory. They are nothing more than indicators, and may be proved wrong by subsequent experience. But if the Western church is to survive, it needs to look for whatever hints are available to it. The following, then, are offered with caution.

1. The above models all place a high premium on *relationship*. Western society under the ravages of individualism incubates a hunger for meaningful relationships. Church communities must be careful to allow time and space for relating, and not permit programme or structure to squeeze it out.

2. In discussion with such groups, the words *honesty* and *reality* come up often. People are tired of false claims to happiness or success. They would rather hear an honest story of failure than a trumped-up 'testimony' of God's power at work. The ambiguity and brokenness of life is simply too obvious to be glossed over.

3. There is *minimal structure* in experimental ventures. High degrees of organization are regarded as stifling of creativity. The institutional basis of the church, and even the professionalism of the clergy is regarded with suspicion.

4. Attempts are made to *connect* the worship and faith life of the community with the everyday cultural experience of the participants. Language, symbols and rituals are drawn as much from the relevant culture as they are from the tradition of the church.

5. The communities are *open* in every sense of the word. Open to new people, open to God, open to new experiences, open to changing direction, open to suffering. There is a spirit of adventure within them, and little of the judgement, inflexibility and power-games that mar church life.

6. These groups are *dynamically ecumenical*. Not in the historical context of the ecumenical movement, but in the sense of hanging very loose from whatever denominational tradition they may participate in, and building friendships with any who share similar visions, either inside or outside the church.

7. An attempt is made to *express mission* in some form or other. There is a recognition that this is an integral part of worshipping God, and that the neglect of mission would be in some sense a betrayal of the nature of congregation.

8. Participants *laugh* and *cry* often in the setting of their community. They are able to laugh freely and frequently because they are also prepared to share in each other's suffering. Human emotion is welcomed and celebrated, with a very loose sense of propriety.

9. *Scripture* is respected and allowed to speak, but not in a remote or disengaged fashion. The attempt is made to relate it to the complex realities of everyday life. The approach to the Bible is inductive and often topical.

10. The *surrounding culture* is taken seriously not only as a mission field, but as a potential source of God's activity. Films are watched, books read, newspapers scanned and artists listened to in the attempt to hear the voice of God.

11. Little importance is placed on *buildings*. This is not because environment is seen as unimportant, but rather that buildings and their maintenance can place an impossible burden on a community. Venues are chosen for how they enhance people's relating to one another.

12. Many of the ventures are *relatively small* in historical terms. They are wary of growing to a size where the relationships which they value so much may be inhibited. Some of the functions of these communities would not be possible in larger groups.

13. There is an appreciation of and encouragement toward *genuine spirituality*, recognizing that traditional patterns may not always be appropriate in the new world. There is a willingness to draw from whatever sources may be helpful.

14. Such communities provide *space* and *refuge* for those who may be battered by the experiences of life. Demands are not placed on participants which they are not ready to meet. Grace is extended so that people may find their own way forward.

15. In certain respects, the communities are *counter-cultural*. They have a commitment to move beyond complicity with the Western values of materialism and individualism, and instead demonstrate some of the qualities of Jesus and his kingdom.

These, then, may be symptoms of the emerging church. There are of course others, and the list makes no claim to be exhaustive. As we map out the new territory which confronts us, it will be necessary for many voices to be listened to. In the dialogue, we may find the whisper of the Spirit leading us on.

12

Conclusion

-

This book began in grief at the deathly situation of the Western church. The intention is that it should end in hope. The communities surveyed in the previous chapter are witness to the new shoots beginning to emerge from the blackened earth.[1] But it would be a mistake to make a pragmatic leap from the introduction to the conclusion; or in theological terms, from the crucifixion to the resurrection. It is not possible to bypass grief without repression. Major sections of the Christian church in the West have not yet begun to recognize the crisis they are immersed in. For them there will be many dark and despairing days before the dawn comes.

The grieving is an essential part of transformation. Too many Christians are looking for strategic or structural solutions, convinced that if they stumble upon the right formula or movement, all will be well. But the deep reinterpretation of the Christian movement necessary to this age has as its precondition the spiritual anguish of confessing failure. Only in the relinquishment of self-assurance, pride and confidence will there be humility to learn from the Spirit.

We must discover the courage of Peter, when faced with his seemingly impossible dilemma – to obey the Spirit or be faithful to Scripture. A tradition which is as inevitably tied to history as the Judaeo-Christian one has great difficulty in making way for genuinely new acts of God. But true theology has always been responsive, in terms of adjusting to the progressive revelation of God. We stand together at a major threshold; there can be no turning back once God has made a way ahead.

Peter was forced to think outside the square, and that is the challenge to the contemporary church. We must be wary of assuming that we know where we are heading and what God has for us as we enter the third millennium. All the analogies of journey, and the people of faith as a pilgrim community, will be newly relevant to us. The number of certainties to be relied on will probably decrease, and we may be forced to let go of some concepts which have given us great security in the past. Above all we need a commitment to flexibility and faithfulness to God, and a new appreciation of the gift of discernment.

The world is not the same one as the thoroughly modern and secular realm of the 1950s. For a while it seemed that the question was how we would incorporate the huge number of changes within the framework of modernity, without suffering 'future shock'. Now it is apparent that the very framework which we used to catalogue the changes is itself crumbling, and the emergent worldview is startlingly different. There are elements of the new culture which will be repugnant to Christians, but there are elements which will provide a home for the gospel. This has always been the situation in the myriad cultures which have hosted Christianity.

The church in the West is in the early stages of a massive reformation. Out on the frontiers there are pioneers of the faith, already engaging with the emerging culture. They are learning as they go, responding to new questions and experiences. The reports they send back from the front lines are vital to the reshaping of the tradition. These are the scouts and trailblazers who will make a way for us, some at the cost of their own lives or ministries. But it is not enough for a few radicals to lead the way. The great mass of the Western church must shift, and it is to that task that this book is dedicated.

In the process, some central Christian resources will have to be reassessed. Scripture will remain central, but the way it is processed and appropriated may need to change. Holiness, worship, spirituality, conversion, evangelism and the shape of the church will be revisited. Radical surgery is more traumatic than minor surgery. It requires careful preparation, skilful intervention and extensive aftercare. But so long as it is the Spirit guiding the process, and not a self-selected group who 'know what's right' for the church, we may retain confidence in the long-term prognosis.

The essence of the church has always been mission. It is created by mission, renewed by mission, and participates in mission. That mission belongs to God, and the church has stakes in it only insofar as it shares the life of God through Christ. To take part in God's mission to the world is to become a conductor of the divine energy which has been unleashed through the tearing open of the Trinity. Apart from involvement in mission, the church becomes a tawdry relic; a dusty museum of religion, suitable for tourists and historians, but little else.

The creeping temptation of the church is to believe that it is an end in itself. Power, wealth, security and the desire for continuity dog the life of the established church as they do any other institution. The characteristics of the God made known in Jesus – love, vulnerability, redemptive suffering, service – are not nearly so attractive. So it is that theology and praxis must continually struggle against the tendency to co-opt God to the agenda of the church, rather than shape the church according to the will of God. Such is the history of the people of God, who attempt to follow the moving pillar of fire.

God will not be contained. The attempt to construct boxes for the divine presence is doomed to tragedy. Those who invest their lives in such misguided pursuits will be left with splinters and the distant laugh of the Spirit. God is God, or even better, God is who God will be. It is no denial of the centrality of Christ to say that we are still finding out who God will be. Christian faith is not a deposit of information, but a relationship with a partner who is constantly luring and dancing in the direction of the horizon. Many groups have assumed that they know the mind and intent of God, and been made to look silly as they clutch their supposed certainties while God moves on.

These are exciting times to be alive in. The West is

undergoing massive cultural transition, which opens new possibilities and perspectives. For those of us in the family of faith, the crisis of the church means that it can no longer continue as it is, and so reformation is a necessity. Furthermore, it may well be that God, as in the time of Cornelius, is doing something new amongst us that we have hardly yet got wind of. All of these factors give an edge of danger and adventure to the calling to discipleship. Following Jesus has regained the urgency and immediacy which belongs to it.

There will be conflict. Cultural systems and deeply held religious convictions are in contention in ways which might have spawned wars in other ages.[2] But conflict and pain are not always to be avoided or suppressed, contrary to current orthodoxy. Birth is a messy process. There is unbelievable anguish and the spray of blood on the walls before the new life arrives, fresh and breathing. It is the cost of life. The alternative to birth is not preservation or continuity, however; it is death. The movement of God is the movement from death to life, and those who would follow are asked to make the same commitment.

It is rather easy to write a book. It is not so easy to follow Christ; to live the story in community with other followers; to engage with the mission of God to the world in the power of the Spirit. I honestly do not know if the church in the West has the ability to make the transitions which this book calls for. If it were up to us alone, I would be pessimistic. My faith is in the God who brings life to the valley of dry bones. This God is able to do that which for us is not possible. Because of this alone, I have utter confidence that faith will be found in the West in the third millennium.

Notes

—

Introduction: Sick to Death

1. Walter Brueggemann, *The Prophetic Imagination*, Philadelphia, Fortress Press, 1978.
2. Tom Sine notes that it is 'the unusual religious organization or church that makes any effort to anticipate tomorrow's needs, challenges, or opportunities'. *Wild Hope: Crises Facing the Human Community on the Threshold of the 21st Century*, Dallas, Word Publishing, 1991, p. 6.
3. David B. Barrett (ed.), *World Christian Encyclopedia: A Comparative survey of Churches and Religions in the Modern World AD 1900–2000*, Nairobi, Oxford University Press, 1982, p. 7.
4. See Loren B. Mead, *The Once and Future Church: Reinventing the Congregation for a New Mission Frontier*, New York, Alban Institute, 1991, pp. 32–5.
5. Henri Nouwen, *The Wounded Healer: Ministry in Contemporary Society*, New York, Doubleday, 1972, pp. 88f.
6. Eugene Peterson, *Working the Angles: The Shape of Pastoral Integrity*, Grand Rapids, MI, Eerdmans, 1987. Says Peterson: 'The pastors of America have metamorphosed into a company of shopkeepers, and the shops they keep are churches. They are preoccupied with shopkeeper's concerns – how to keep the customers happy, how to lure customers away from competitors down the street, how to package the goods so that the customers will lay out more money' (p. 2).
7. 'Among the leaders of today's generation, there is an insistent and growing belief that Christianity is irrelevant. Modern western thinking, it is said, has largely been dominated by Christian values, and these must therefore have contributed to our present predicament . . . Christianity is very firmly perceived as part of the old order, and therefore something to be discarded rather than trusted for the future.' John Drane, *Evangelism for a New Age: Creating Churches for the Next Century*, London, Marshall Pickering, 1994, pp. 14f.
8. Lesslie Newbigin, *The Gospel in a Pluralist Society*, Grand Rapids, MI, Eerdmans, 1989.

176

9. 'Like an aging dowager, living in a decaying mansion on the edge of town, bankrupt and penniless, house decaying around her but acting as if her family still controlled the city, our theologians and church leaders continued to act and think as if we were in charge, as if the old arrangements were still valid.' Stanley Hauerwas and William H. Willimon, *Resident Aliens: Life in the Christian Colony*, Nashville, Abingdon, 1992, p. 29.

10. See John B. Cobb, *Christ in a Pluralistic Age*, Philadelphia, Westminster Press, 1975.

11. John Drane, *What is the New Age Saying to the Church?*, London, Marshall Pickering, 1991, p. 239.

12. 'This evolution has been going on unconsciously throughout human history. That explains why civilization has progressed and why humans have grown larger, lived longer and so forth. Now, however, we are making the whole process conscious. That is what the Manuscript is telling us. That is what this movement toward a worldwide spiritual consciousness is all about.' James Redfield, *The Celestine Prophecy: An Adventure*, Sydney, Bantam Books, 1993, p. 121.

13. 'Yet in most cases, people are not turning to the church to satisfy this hunger; instead, many are turning to some expression of the New Age.' Dave Tomlinson, *The Post-Evangelical*, London, Triangle, 1995, p. 141.

14. Neill notes that 'In 1800 it was still by no means certain that Christianity would be successful in turning itself into a universal religion.' By the end of the century there were Christian converts from 'every race, every religion, every social level, and every form of human organization.' Stephen Neill, *A History of Christian Missions*, Harmondsworth, Penguin, 1964, pp. 243–60.

15. Bosch quotes P. Schutz as protesting: 'The house of the church is on fire! In our missionary outreach we resemble a lunatic who carries the harvest into his burning barn.' Bosch explains: 'Schutz located the problem not "outside", on the mission field, but in the heart of the Western church itself.' David J. Bosch, *Transforming Mission: Paradigm Shifts in Theology of Mission*, Maryknoll, NY, Orbis Books, 1991, p. 5.

16. Barrett, *World Christian Encyclopedia*, p. 7.

17. Emil Brunner, *The Word and the World*, New York, Charles Scribner's Sons, 1931, p. 108.

18. 'First and supremely it is God who exists for the world. And since the community of Jesus Christ exists first and supremely for God, it has no option but in its own manner and place to exist for the

world.' Karl Barth, *Church Dogmatics*, IV, 3, pt. 2, trans. G. W. Bromiley, Edinburgh, T. & T. Clark, 1962, p. 762.

19. See the illustrative story related by Peter and Sue Kaldor in their aptly titled book, *Where the River Flows: Sharing the Gospel in Contemporary Australia*, Homebush West, NSW, Lancer Books, 1988, p. xxiii.

20. 'A few may still believe that by electing a few "Christian" senators, passing a few new laws, and tinkering with the federal budget we can form a "Christian" culture, or at least one that is a bit more just. But most people know this view to be touchingly anachronistic. All sorts of Christians are waking up and realizing that it is no longer "our world" – if it ever was.' Hauerwas and Willimon, *Resident Aliens*, p. 16.

21. 'The Christian life of theologians, churches and human beings is faced more than ever today with a double crisis: the *crisis of relevance* and the *crisis of identity*.' Jürgen Moltmann, *The Crucified God: The Cross of Christ as the Foundation and Criticism of Christian Theology*, London, SCM, 1974, p. 7.

1: Acts 10 – Outside the Box

1. 'Luke has selected and composed his materials to describe how the disciples bore their witness to the gospel "in Jerusalem, and in all Judea and Samaria, and to the ends of the earth" (Acts 1.8). He tells of how the church changed from being predominantly Jewish to becoming increasingly Gentile.' World Council of Churches, *Spirit, Gospel, Cultures: Bible Studies on the Acts of the Apostles*, Geneva, WCC Publications, 1995, p. 2.

2. John Stott notes Luke's 'emphasis on the Spirit', commenting: 'In the early chapters of the Acts Luke refers to the promise, the gift, the baptism, the power and the fullness of the Spirit in the experience of God's people.' *The Spirit, The Church and The World: The Message of Acts*, Downers Grove, ILL, IVP, 1990, p. 60.

3. 'The New Testament writers were not scholars who had the leisure to research the evidence before they put pen to paper. Rather, they wrote in the context of an "emergency situation", of a church which, because of its missionary encounter with the world, was *forced* to theologize.' David Bosch, *Transforming Mission: Paradigm Shifts in Theology of Mission*, Maryknoll, NY, Orbis, 1991, p. 16.

4. 'The importance of the story for Luke and Luke's book is thus

unmistakable. It marks the final critical stage in the extension of the Gospel and the expansion of the church.' C. K. Barrett, *A Critical and Exegetical Commentary on the Acts of the Apostles*, Edinburgh, T. & T. Clark, 1994, p. 491. Willimon says of the Peter and Cornelius story in Acts: 'Judged solely on the basis of the amount of space Luke gives to the story, we know that we are dealing with a crucial concern of Acts, a pivot for the entire book, a turning point in the long drama of redemption.' William H. Willimon, *Acts: Interpretation – A Bible Commentary for Teaching and Preaching*, Atlanta, John Knox Press, 1988, p. 95.

5. Stott notes: 'It is difficult for us to grasp the impassable gulf which yawned in those days between the Jews on the one hand and the Gentiles (including even the "God-fearers") on the other.' Stott, *The Spirit, the Church and the World*, p. 185.

6. See I. H. Marshall, *The Acts of the Apostles*, Sheffield, Sheffield Academic Press, 1992, pp. 71f.

7. See Stott, who explains: 'No orthodox Jew would ever enter the home of a Gentile, even a God-fearer, or invite such into his home ...' Stott, *The Spirit, the Church and the World*, p. 185.

8. Barrett says of the Jewish church's reticence toward outsiders: 'God overruled their objection and himself brought the Gentiles in.' Barrett, *A Critical and Exegetical Commentary on the Acts of the Apostles*, p. 491.

9. Hymn 335, 'We Limit Not the Truth of God', G. Rawson, *The Baptist Hymn Book*, London, Psalms and Hymns Trust, 1962.

2: The Beckoning God

1. See Benjamin Tonna, *Gospel for the Cities: A Socio-Theology of Urban Mission*, trans. W. E. Jerman, Maryknoll, NY, Orbis, 1982, pp. 7f.: 'If the Lord is with us, signs of his active presence cannot fail to be present.'

2. 'The situation is, therefore, quite new. It represents a veritable uncharted sea for theology, where neither the menacing rocks nor the clear channels are known ...' Langdon Gilkey, *Society and the Sacred: Toward a Theology of Culture in Decline*, New York, Crossroad, 1981, p. 13.

3. Letty Russell has introduced the category of partnership as a central motif to theology. See *The Future of Partnership*, Philadelphia, Westminster Press, 1979.

4. As published in *Baptist Times*, John Drane, 'Was God in Dunblane?', 21 March 1996, p. 8.

5. Ernest Kurtz quotes a *New York Times* religion writer, who reports that a clergy member said of the AA group meeting in his church building: 'There is more spirituality in this building on Tuesday evenings in the basement than on Sunday mornings in the sanctuary.' 'Twelve Step Programs', pp. 277–302 in Peter H. Van Ness (ed.), *Spirituality and the Secular Quest*, London, SCM, 1996, p. 277.

6. Hymn 576 'Great is Thy Faithfulness', by T. O. Chisholm, in *The Baptist Hymn Book*, London, Psalms and Hymns Trust, 1962.

7. See Norman Pittenger, *Unbounded Love: God and Man in Process*, New York, Seabury Press, 1976, p. 25, where he notes that Christian theology began to develop ideas 'not derived from Jewish religion' but more from 'speculative views of philosophers who talked about "first cause" or "absolute being" and on the uncriticized portrayal of dictatorial control, sheerly omnipotent power, or tyrannical rule which they saw in the governments of the petty states of the then-known world roundabout the Mediterranean basin.'

8. 'Christian faith stands and falls with the knowledge of the crucified Christ, that is, with the knowledge of God *in* the crucified Christ, or, to use Luther's even bolder phrase, with the knowledge of the "crucified God".' Jürgen Moltmann, *The Crucified God: The Cross of Christ as the Foundation and Criticism of Christian Theology*, trans. R. A. Wilson and J. Bowden, London, SCM, 1974, p. 65.

9. John V. Taylor notes that: 'The anthropomorphic metaphors do not contradict the transcendence or the incorporeality of this God. The absolute veto against making any image of him was meant to ensure that verbal imagery would not be intepreted literally.' *The Christlike God*, London, SCM, 1992, p. 149.

10. See John Knox, *The Humanity and Divinity of Christ: A Study of Pattern in Christology*, Cambridge, Cambridge University Press, 1967, pp. 5–9.

11. Drane, 'Was God in Dunblane?'

12. Hans Küng, *The Church*, trans. R. and R. Ockenden, London, SCM, 1968, pp. 24–9.

13. 'I believe that the proper idiom for the prophet in cutting through the royal numbness and denial is the *language of grief*, the rhetoric that engages the community in mourning for a funeral they do not want to admit.' Brueggemann, *The Prophetic Imagination*, p. 51.

14. See Brueggemann, *The Prophetic Imagination*, pp. 62–79.

3: The Bible and Beyond

1. See Dave Tomlinson, *The Post-Evangelical*, London, Triangle, 1995, pp. 105–9.

2. John L. McKenzie asserts: 'No other ancient religion conceived the relation of deity and worshippers in positive terms founded upon a collective act of the people which could be located in space and dated in time.' *A Theology of the Old Testament*, New York, Image Books, 1976, p. 77. John Drane notes: 'The central feature of this awesome occasion [Sinai] was the commitment that God made to Israel, and the obligations that Israel accepted in return.' *Introducing the Old Testament*, Oxford, Lynx, 1987, pp. 51f.

3. 'The exile was in many ways a watershed for the people of Israel ... Prayer and the reading of the Old Testament Law and prophets came to be all important.' Drane, *Introducing the Old Testament*, pp. 303f. 'Somewhere, then, before the completion of the Torah about the middle of the fourth century BC, and the Maccabean Revolt in 167 BC there took place a subtle transfer of emphasis from the Temple to the Torah which was yet to be of momentous importance for the life of Judaism.' D. S. Russell, *Between the Testaments*, London, SCM, 1960, p. 44.

4. D. S. Russell says: 'Throughout the whole of this period, however, they stood as a bulwark against the encroachments of Hellenism by showing themselves to be doughty champions of Torah religion.' *Between the Testaments*, p. 50.

5. See Ralph P. Martin, *New Testament Foundations: A Guide for Christian Students*, vol. I, *The Four Gospels*, Exeter, The Paternoster Press, 1975, p. 86.

6. Edwin D. Freed reports that 'the Pharisees were concerned with sabbath observance, that they subscribed to an oral Torah, "the tradition of the elders" (Mark 7.3, 5), that they observed laws of ceremonial purity, especially when eating, and that they did not associate with people not observing such laws'. *The New Testament: A Critical Introduction*, Belmont, CA, Wadsworth, 1986, p. 17.

7. Thus Rudolf Bultmann claims: 'That Jesus did not polemically contest the authority of the Old Testament is proven by the course later taken by his Church ...' *Theology of the New Testament*, vol. I, trans. K. Grobel, London, SCM, 1952, p. 16.

8. 'He did not die through chance or misfortune, but died by the law as one who was "reckoned with transgressors" (Luke 22.37), because he was condemned as a "blasphemer" by the guardians of the law and of the faith.' Moltmann, *The Crucified God*, p. 133.

9. Athol Gill, *The Fringes of Freedom: Following Jesus, Living Together, Working for Justice*, Homebush West, NSW, Lancer, 1990, p. 27.

10. See Joachim Jeremias, *New Testament Theology*, vol. I, *The Proclamation of Jesus*, trans. J. Bowden, London, SCM, 1971. He asserts that only when one accepts Jesus' commitment to the Old Testament 'can one assess what it means that Jesus should venture to make more radical, to criticize, indeed to supersede words of the *Torah*' (p. 206).

11. 'The antithesis really implied in the language is between an external law, written in a book or on tables of stone, and the dictates of the inward moral sense informed by true knowledge of God.' J. Skinner, *Prophecy and Religion: Studies in the Life of Jeremiah*, Cambridge, Cambridge University Press, 1951, p. 331.

12. 'That people are more or less religiously inclined, if true, might well be a good thing. But those who really have faith will never regard their faith as an actualization or expression of their religious life. Instead they will confess that their religious capacity as such would have led them to gods and idols but in no way to Jesus Christ.' Karl Barth, Lecture on 'The Knowledge of God', as quoted in R. J. Erler and R. Marquard (eds.), *A Karl Barth Reader*, trans. G. W. Bromiley, Grand Rapids MI, Eerdmans, 1986, pp. 37f.

13. Fyodor Dostoevsky, *The Brothers Karamazov*, trans. A. H. MacAndrew, New York, Bantam, 1981, p. 307.

14. 'The Church as institution is characterized by endurance, stability, and by the rules of the game followed by its members. It runs the risk of losing the beat of history, of stagnating, of forgetting its primary function of service, of fostering passivity, monotony, mechanization, and alienation.' Leonardo Boff, *Church: Charisma and Power – Liberation Theology and the Institutional Church*, trans J. W. Diercksmeier, London, SCM, 1985, p. 48.

15. See discussion on this issue in Tomlinson, *The Post-Evangelical*, pp. 109–22.

16. Paul Tillich says in relation to Scripture: 'A collection of assumed divine revelations concerning "faith and morals" without a revelatory event which they interpret is a lawbook with divine authorization, but it is not the Word of God, and it has no revelatory power.' *Systematic Theology: I – Reason and Revelation, Being and God*, London, SCM, 1978, p. 125.

17. See James Dunn, *Christology in the Making: An Inquiry into the Origins of the Doctrine of the Incarnation*, London, SCM, 1980, pp. 239–50: 'However much the human encounter with God had

been experienced as personal address, it had not been conceived in terms of a person distinct from God. But now in John the word of God is identified with a particular historical person, whose pre-existence as a person with God is asserted throughout' (p. 250).

18. See Lesslie Newbigin, *Foolishness to the Greeks: The Gospel and Western Culture*, Geneva, World Council of Churches, 1986, pp. 45f.
19. See Drane, *Evangelism for a New Age*, p. 36.
20. Augustine of Hippo, *In Epistolam ad Parthos*, tractatus 7, sect. 8, AD 413.

4: The Weariness of the Church

1. Jürgen Moltmann, *The Open Church: Invitation to a Messianic Lifestyle*, London, SCM, 1978, pp. 19–26.
2. Moltmann, *The Open Church*, p. 24.
3. Quoted in Roland Howard, *The Rise and Fall of the Nine O'Clock Service: A Cult within the Church?*, London, Mowbray, 1996, p. 141.
4. Howard, *The Rise and Fall of the Nine O'Clock Service*, p. 142.
5. Athol Gill, *The Fringes of Freedom: Following Jesus, Living Together, Working for Justice*, Homebush West, NSW, Lancer, 1990, pp. 52f.
6. See in particular Letty Russell, *The Future of Partnership*, Philadelphia, Westminster Press, 1979, and *Growth in Partnership*, Philadelphia, Westminster Press, 1981.
7. Scott Peck, *The Different Drum: Community Making and Peace*, New York, Simon & Schuster, 1988, pp. 72f.
8. James K. Baxter, 'The Moon and the Chestnut Tree', *Jerusalem Daybook*, Wellington, Price Milburn, 1971, p. 17.
9. For the contemporary translation, I cite the version in Gill's *The Fringes of Freedom*, pp. 30f.

5: Holiness – Above and Apart

1. Political correctness notwithstanding, the appellations 'Old' and 'New' carry real significance in marking the importance of Jesus for Christian theology.
2. Note Eugene Petersen's translation of John 1.14: 'The Word became flesh and blood, and moved into the neighbourhood.' *The Message: The New Testament in Contemporary English*, Colorado, NavPress, 1993, p. 185.

3. See John G. Gammie, *Holiness in Israel*, Minneapolis, Fortress, 1989, pp. 9–70.

4. 'Holiness demands separation ... The notion of separation is pervasive in the priestly traditions of the Bible from the Book of Genesis onward.' Gammie, *Holiness in Israel*, p. 9.

5. J. C. Ryle, *Holiness: Its Nature, Hindrances, Difficulties, and Roots*, London, James Clarke & Co, 1952, p. 36.

6. John Barker, *This is the Will of God: A Study in the Doctrine of Entire Sanctification as a Definite Experience*, London, Epworth, 1956, pp. 88f.

7. Ryle, *Holiness*, p. 53.

8. Discussion at greater depth would require consideration of the 'ethical' use of *kosmos* in the New Testament, which might be better translated 'system'. See J. A. T. Robinson, *On Being the Church in the World*, London, Mowbrays, 1977, pp. 19–22.

9. *The Fringes of Freedom*, p. 23.

10. Moltmann, *The Open Church*, p. 55.

11. Moltmann, *The Open Church*, p. 107.

12. Pete Ward, *Growing Up Evangelical: Youthwork and the Making of a Subculture*, London, SPCK, 1996, p. 161.

13. Drane, *Evangelism for a New Age*, p. 188.

6: Dreaming the Forbidden Dream

1. See Paulo Freire, *Pedagogy of the Oppressed*, Harmondsworth, Penguin, 1972, pp. 22f.

2. Walter Brueggemann, *The Prophetic Imagination*, p. 44.

3. Brueggemann, *The Prophetic Imagination*, p. 59.

4. Gill, *The Fringes of Freedom*, p. 105.

5. Brueggemann, *The Prophetic Imagination*, p. 63.

6. Langdon Gilkey, *Reaping the Whirlwind: A Christian Interpretation of History*, New York, Seabury, 1981, pp. 47–57.

7. Douglas Coupland, *Polaroids from the Dead*, New York, Regan Books, 1996, p. 156.

8. Carl Gustav Jung, *Memories, Dreams and Reflections*, trans. R. and C. Winston, London, Fontana, 1967, pp. 52–6.

9. Jung, *Memories, Dreams and Reflections*, p. 57.

10. Note Pannenberg's view of the proleptic nature of Jesus' resurrection, with the significance that the end of history has occurred within history. Wolfhart Pannenberg, *Jesus – God and Man*, trans. L. L. Wilkins and D. A. Priebe, London, SCM, 1968, pp. 53–108.

11. For an interesting discussion of 'reframing', see Michael Frost, *Jesus the Fool*, Sutherland NSW, Albatross, 1994, pp. 70–85.
12. I am indebted to my friend and colleague, the Rev Ian Brown, Chief Executive Officer of the Baptist Union of New Zealand, for this illustration.
13. Jürgen Moltmann, *Theology of Hope: On the Ground and the Implications of a Christian Eschatology*, trans. J. Leitch, London, SCM, 1967, p. 21.

7: The Emerging World

1. Walter Truett Anderson, *Reality Isn't What It Used To Be: Theatrical Politics, Ready-to-Wear Religion, Global Myths, Primitive Chic, and Other Wonders of the Postmodern World*, San Francisco, Harper & Row, 1990, p. 3.
2. Quoted in Mike Featherstone, *Consumer Culture and Postmodernism*, London, Sage, 1991, p. 1.
3. Ernst Gellner, *Postmodernism, Reason and Religion*, London, Routledge, 1992, p. 22.
4. Jaques Derrida, *Of Grammatology*, trans. G. C. Spivak, Baltimore, Johns Hopkins University Press, 1976; and *Speech and Phenomena and Other Essays on Husserl's Theory of Signs*, trans. D. B. Allison, Evanston, Northwestern University Press, 1973; Jean François Lyotard, *The Postmodern Condition: A Report on Knowledge*, trans. G. Bennington and B. Massumi, Manchester, Manchester University Press, 1984; Jean Baudrillard, *The Mirror of Production*, trans. M. Poster, St Louis, Telos Press, 1975; and *Simulations*, trans. P. Foss, P. Patton and P. Bleitchman, New York, Semiotext(e), 1983; Richard Rorty, *Philosophy and the Mirror of Nature*, Princeton, Princeton University Press, 1979; and *Contingency, Irony, and Solidarity*, Cambridge, Cambridge University Press, 1989.
5. See, for example, Walter Truett Anderson, *Reality Isn't What It Used To Be: Theatrical Politics, Ready-to-Wear Religion, Global Myths, Primitive Chic, and Other Wonders of the Postmodern World*, San Francisco, Harper & Row, 1990; Steven Connor, *Postmodernist Culture: An Introduction to Theories of the Contemporary*, Oxford, Blackwell, 1989; John Docker, *Postmodernism and Popular Culture: A Cultural History*, Cambridge, Cambridge University Press, 1994; Mike Featherstone, *Consumer Culture and Postmodernism*, London, Sage, 1991; David Harvey, *The Condition*

of Postmodernity: An Enquiry into the Origins of Cultural Change, Oxford, Blackwell, 1990.

6. See Robert Linthicum, *City of God, City of Satan: A Biblical Theology of the Urban Church*, Grand Rapids, MI, Zondervan, 1991, pp. 17f.

7. 'Further, since the electronic media are most prevalent in the saturation of the self, it is not surprising to see these media, in particular television, playing a formative role in the construction and reconstruction of our self-understandings.' J. R. Middleton and B. J. Walsh, *Truth is Stranger than It Used to Be: Biblical Faith in a Postmodern Age*, Downers Grove, ILL, IVP, 1995, p. 54.

8. See T. Costello, 'The City', pp. 1–10 in T. Costello (ed.), *Ministry in an Urban World: Responding to the City*, Canberra, Acorn Press, 1991, p. 7: 'The constant psychic drain of recognising strangers and dispatching the emotional energy to converse means that urban reserve is really a subconscious survival mechanism.'

9. 'If pluralism relativizes all traditions, it seems to imply that because they are equally good our own choice of values or meanings is arbitrary.' John Cobb, *Christ in a Pluralistic Age*, Philadelphia, Westminster Press, 1975, p. 58.

10. Langdon Gilkey, *Naming the Whirlwind: The Renewal of God Language*, Indianapolis, Bobbs-Merrill, 1969, p. 70.

11. Stephen Toulmin, *Cosmopolis: The Hidden Agenda of Modernity*, New York, Free Press, 1990, pp. 186–92.

12. Stanley Grenz, *A Primer on Postmodernism*, Grand Rapids, MI, Eerdmans, 1996, p. 26.

13. The classic statement of this generational angst is in Douglas Coupland's *Generation X: Tales for an Accelerated Culture*, London, Abacus, 1992.

14. Douglas Coupland, *Life After God*, New York, Pocket Books, 1994, pp. 104f.

15. Coupland, *Life After God*, p. 109.

16. See Howard Rheingold, *The Virtual Community: Finding Connection in a Computerized World*, London, Secker & Warburg, 1994.

17. See, for example, Neil Postman, *Technopoly: The Surrender of Culture to Technology*, New York, Vintage Books, 1993.

18. Rob and Brian Draper, 'Taboo Technology', pp. 21–4 in *Third Way: The Modern World through Christian Eyes*, December 1996, vol. 19, no. 10, p. 22.

19. 'It turns out that beneath the rational surface of the more-or-less secular "realism" that is supposed to be our official worldview – and not too far beneath it, either – lurks a seething cauldron of

cults and faiths of all description.' Anderson, *Reality Isn't What It Used To Be*, p. 187.

20. Drane, *Evangelism for a New Age*, p. 16.
21. 'In the escalating search for road signs on the journey through the desert, many people have found themselves needing "religion," but unable to stomach what much of "organised religion" passes off as religion.' M. Scott Peck, *Further Along the Road Less Travelled: The Unending Journey Toward Spiritual Growth*, New York, Simon & Schuster, 1993, p. 194.
22. Coupland, *Life After God*, p. 359.

8: Beyond the Boundaries

1. See Ward, *Growing Up Evangelical*, esp. pp. 161–85.
2. Discussing Lucan theology, David Bosch notes: 'The Spirit is thus ... not only the initiator and guide of mission, but also the one who empowers to mission.' *Transforming Mission*, p. 114.
3. Moltmann bemoans the obsession with 'the Spirit of redemption' which 'makes people turn away from "this world" and hope for a better world beyond'. In contrast he asserts that 'experience of the life-giving Spirit in the faith of the heart and in the sociality of love leads of itself beyond the limits of the church to the rediscovery of the same Spirit in nature, in plants, in animals, and in the ecosystems of the earth'. Jürgen Moltmann, *The Spirit of Life: A Universal Affirmation*, trans. M. Kohl, London, SCM, 1992, pp. 8–10.
4. See H. H. Rosin, *Missio Dei: An Examination of the Origin, Contents and Function of the Term in Protestant Missiological Discussion*, Leiden, Interuniversity Institute for Missiological and Ecumenical Research, 1972.
5. 'It is not the church that has a mission to fulfil to the world; it is the mission of the Son and the Spirit through the Father that includes the church, creating a church as it goes on its way.' Jürgen Moltmann, *The Church in the Power of the Spirit: A Contribution to Messianic Ecclesiology*, trans. M. Kohl, London, SCM, 1977, p. 64.
6. James K. Baxter, 'Song to the Holy Spirit', *Collected Poems*, ed. J. E. Weir, Wellington, Oxford University Press, 1979, p. 572.
7. See Drane, *Evangelism for a New Age*, pp. 190f.
8. For a brief description of Parallel Universe, see Chapter 11.
9. See T. Lorenzen, *Resurrection and Discipleship: Interpretive*

Models, Biblical Reflections, Theological Consequences, Maryknoll, NY, Orbis, 1995, pp. 284–95.

10. 'It would not have occurred to anyone to affirm that Jesus was human, for the obvious reason that it would not have occurred to anyone that he might have been anything else.' John Knox, *The Humanity and Divinity of Christ: A Study of Pattern in Christology*, Cambridge, Cambridge University Press, 1967, p. 5.

11. John Robinson notes that '... for Paul, too, the solidarity of Christ with our present human condition is of fundamental theological importance'. J. A. T. Robinson, *The Human Face of God*, London, SCM, 1973, p. 53.

12. See Knox, *The Humanity and Divinity of Christ*, pp. 73–92.

13. Moltmann notes that the human person '... suffers because he lives ... This may be called the dialectic of human life: we live because and in so far as we love – and we suffer and die because and in so far as we love.' Moltmann, *The Crucified God*, p. 253.

14. Peck, *Further Along the Road Less Travelled*, p. 158.

9: Spirituality for the Times

1. Drane, *What is the New Age Saying to the Church?*, p. 15.

2. John U'Ren, 'Urban Ministry and Burn Out', pp. 47–62 in Costello (ed.), *Ministry in an Urban World*, p. 53.

3. Henri Nouwen, *Seeds of Hope*, London, Darton, Longman & Todd, 1989, p. 6.

4. 'Compartmentalization is easy. Integrity is painful. But without it there can be no wholeness. Integrity requires that we be fully open to the conflicting forces and ideas and stresses in life.' Peck, *Further Along the Road Less Travelled*, p. 181.

5. See Matthew Fox, *Original Blessing: A Primer in Creation Spirituality Presented in Four Paths, Twenty-six Themes and Two Questions*, Sante Fe, New Mexico, Bear and Co., 1983.

6. Nouwen, *Seeds of Hope*, p. 12.

7. Nouwen, *Seeds of Hope*, p. 65.

8. John Drane suggests three spheres of interaction in relation to evangelism: God's story, Bible stories and personal stories. Drane, *Evangelism for a New Age*, pp. 68–72.

9. 'In this world the question of a rebirth of feasts in culture, of a capacity for play in personal life, and of the power for celebration of free and open liturgies in the representation of Christian freedom and joy is acquiring new importance.' Moltmann, *The Open Church*, p. 65.

10. Frederick Buechner, *Telling Secrets*, San Francisco, HarperSan-Francisco, 1991, p. 3.
11. See Walter Wink, *Engaging the Powers: Discernment and Resistance in a World of Domination*, Minneapolis, Fortress Press, 1992, pp. 164–8.

10: Finding Faith

1. See Gill, *The Fringes of Freedom*, pp. 21f.
2. 'The Gospels make wonderfully clear that the disciples had not the foggiest idea of what they had gotten into when they followed Jesus.' Hauerwas and Willimon, *Resident Aliens*, p. 49.
3. Gill, *The Fringes of Freedom*, p. 39.
4. Gill, *The Fringes of Freedom*, p. 24.
5. Thorwald Lorenzen notes that the Anabaptists 'criticized the reformers' understanding of faith as being superficial and shallow. In their understanding the reformers preached a "sinful sweet Christ", who does not lead to a "betterment of life".' *Resurrection and Discipleship*, p. 233. Lorenzen cites Hans Denck in his statement "none may truly know (Christ) unless he follow after him with his life". *Resurrection and Discipleship*, p. 234, n. 71.
6. Moltmann, *The Open Church*, p. 125.
7. See Dave Andrews, *Building a Better World*, Claremont, CA, Albatross, 1996.
8. For a similar and more systematic application of set theory to models of church, see Paul G. Hiebert, *Anthropological Reflections on Missiological Issues*, Grand Rapids, MI, Baker Books, 1994, pp. 107–36.
9. 'We can only achieve perfect liberty and enjoy fellowship with Jesus when his command, his call to absolute discipleship, is appreciated in its entirety.' Dietrich Bonhoeffer, *The Cost of Discipleship*, trans. R. H. Fuller, London, SCM, 1980, p. 31.
10. Hauerwas and Willimon, *Resident Aliens*, p. 52.
11. J. B. Metz, *The Emergent Church: The Future of Christianity in a Postbourgeois World*, trans. P. Mann, London, SCM, 1981, pp. 14f.
12. See Moltmann, *The Crucified God*, pp. 128–53.
13. Drane, *Evangelism for a New Age*, p. 70.
14. See Connor, *Postmodernist Culture*, pp. 28–30.

11: Models to Hope On

1. Lloyd Geering notes that 'New Zealand has in many respects moved further in the direction of a secular or religiously-neutral state than has been the case with most states of western Europe.' 'Pluralism and the future of religion in New Zealand', pp. 171–84 in B. Colless and P. Donovan (eds.), *Religion in New Zealand Society*, Edinburgh, T. & T. Clark, 1980, p. 176.
2. Duncan Macleod, 'Parallel Universe, Auckland', pp. 1–2 in *Crumbs*, vol. 10, no. 2, Wellington, Methodist & Presbyterian National Youth Ministry Offices, p. 1.
3. Simon Chaplin, 'The Pavement: 3 months reflections on possible urban mission initiatives in inner city Auckland', Unpublished paper, Auckland, 1996, p. 8.
4. Chaplin, 'The Pavement', pp. 12f.
5. Chaplin, 'The Pavement', p. 14.

12: Conclusion

1. Atholl Gill uses the words of novelist Morris West in *Clowns of God* as a basis to speak of the emerging church: 'So, in the evil times which are now upon us, you are chosen to keep the small flame of love alight, to nurture the seeds of goodness in this small place, until the day when the Spirit sends you out to light other candles in a dark land and plant new seeds in a blackened earth.' *Fringes of Freedom*, p. 82.
2. See Tom Sine, *Cease Fire: Searching for Sanity in America's Culture Wars*, Grand Rapids, MI, Eerdmans, 1995. 'Culture wars not only precede shooting wars but also provoke them' (p. 2).

Index